I0541729

Dark
Valleys

Reflections of God Moments : Book 11

Dedication

Walking through challenges invokes a stronger person than you think you are. This book is dedicated to my aunts who I have watched from a distance as they navigated personal loss and held onto God's unchanging hand. Sharon, Beth, Judy and Bonnie, you are loved and appreciated. Your journey has taught me and I have grown watching you navigate the tides of life. Grateful to know my family legacy is strong.

Dark Valleys
Reflections of God Moments Book 11
copyright © 2025

All rights reserved. No part of this book may be reproduced or utilized in any form or by any means, electronic or mechanical, including photocopying, recording, or by any information storage and retrieval system, without written permission from the publisher.

All Scripture quotations are taken from The Message, copyright © 1993, 2002, 2018 by Eugene H. Peterson. Used by permission of NavPress. All rights reserved. Represented by Tyndale House Publishers.

Scripture taken from the New King James Version®. Copyright © 1982 by Thomas Nelson. Used by permission. All rights reserved.

Written by: Donesa Walker
Design by: Will Baten
Edited by: Kelley Inderman

Contents

Be prepared. You're up against far more than you can handle on your own. Take all the help you can get, every weapon God has issued, so that when it's all over but the shouting you'll still be on your feet. Truth, righteousness, peace, faith, and salvation are more than words. Learn how to apply them. You'll need them throughout your life. God's Word is an indispensable weapon. In the same way, prayer is essential in this ongoing warfare. Pray hard and long. Pray for your brothers and sisters. Keep your eyes open. Keep each other's spirits up so that no one falls behind or drops out.

Ephesians 6: 13-18

Spirit Warfare!

Numbness is the feeling when emotions have deserted you, when the trial is deep and the road you have been on that is ahead is long, and when you are bone weary. In 2018, after trip after trip back to the hospital, my spirit was tired and weary. I had no ability to fight anymore and was ready to let go and surrender to the infection raging in my body. I was septic with repeated abscesses in my guts from a simple surgical procedure gone wrong. I was tired. I was bone weary and spirit flagging done. But, God had a different plan. He renewed His Spirit within me to keep on and a well rose up within me to keep going. My husband tells me that he knows the day it happened because it was a stark change in my progress. It was the day I began to fight again. When things don't go our way and we pray for answers, miracles and resolutions but they do not appear to come in a timely manner, we become disillusioned and disappointed. Our spirits fail, our emotions fail, our will fails and then we become numb. That quiet place is the valley of death. In Psalms, David says, yea, though I walk through the valley of death...Your rod and staff comfort me. This is important to understand. This place of darkness and defeat is a battle you are prepared for but requires the quiet, the numb, the depths because it is a place of the impossible becoming possible. For some this is the death of a loved one, for others it is the death of a dream, a life ambition or a loss of high value. In Ephesians, Paul instructs the church to be prepared. We are up against far more than we can handle on our own and we must use every weapon that God has issued for this battle so that when it is over, we will still be on our feet. These weapons: truth, peace, faith, righteousness, and salvation are more than mere words or concepts.

They are weapons that we must learn to wield in the fiercest of battles. God's word is the indispensable sword of spirit warfare. Prayer is essential and staying alert while encouraging others is critical. Battles are not fun. They are brutal. They rip and tear at your soul. These battles come in all shapes and sizes. It is a vicious fight to the finish with the prince of the power of the air. When battles look like they are carnal and they seem to be impossible, these are the conditions where the ground is ripe for victory but we cannot give up. We have to take the initiative and gear up for the battles that are fierce. What starts in one area ends in another as these battles are not of flesh and blood, though they appear to be so. Loss is hard. Loss of dreams, loss of love, loss of life, loss of hope, loss of investment, and loss of emotional desire are all intense battlefields of the mind, heart and soul. Numbness is the place of the valley, the gathering of resources for the climb back into the battle. Be prepared. Speak the word. Pray the Spirit and Encourage others despite your circumstances. This battle isn't yours alone. It is His. He is the champion. Stand strong and see that He is good.

Those who had seen it told the others what had happened to the demon possessed man and the pigs. At first they were in awe—and then they were upset, upset over the drowned pigs. They demanded that Jesus leave and not come back.

Mark 5: 16-17

Upset Awe!

I have seen many storms in my life and their power is awesome to observe. From lightning strikes to swirling winds, to hail storms, to snowstorms, to tornadoes. The awe brought by the storm soon changes to upset and frustration when it impacts lifestyle and limits resources. I remember a few years ago, what we call Snowmageddon here. It started with warnings of course which were mostly ignored because snow here is a rarity and barely lasts. Snow here shuts everything down so the only thing people thought was, we get a day off. The snow began to fall heavy and wet, so beautiful a blanket but then it kept falling. The temps began to plummet and suddenly panic ensued. The beauty of snowfall and a day off suddenly had more serious consequences. Pipes freezing and bursting, roofs collapsing, no food/water, store shelves empty and no electricity suddenly spelled disaster rather than awe. The miracle of the snowfall had become a bitter pill to swallow. Storms like these in our lives can quickly change our awe to an upset as disaster and lifestyle change can be demonstrated. In this story, a man possessed by devils terrorized the city and Jesus comes into the situation. He commands the devils to leave the man, inspiring awe and miraculous wonder but then the demons were sent into the pigs and the pigs, which were the income makers, dove off the cliff impacting their pocketbooks. Now, the miracle has become a disaster to the people. They had the miracle worker in their midst but they asked him to leave because their finances were impacted. How many times in our lives have we overlooked or missed out on the miracle because we were impacted in other ways? How many times has our awe turned to upset because things didn't go as expected? The miracle of awe became a loss for a whole village of people because they didn't focus on the miracle worker, but the act. They lost sight of the truth due to their reality. This has happened in so many lives. Time after time I have seen people lose sight of God because their circumstances changed. The children of Israel did this over and over. They experienced the miracle of deliverance from slavery but lost hope when they approached the Red Sea. How quickly they lost sight of the God of miracles when their circumstances looked impossible. Then God steps up to perform the Red Sea miracle but as quickly as they are delivered in awe to the other side, they lost focus again as they looked around at their circumstances and saw the limitations. Over and over this happens and is still happening in our lives. We lose sight of the Miracle Worker because we focus on our circumstances rather than on Who He Is. I am so guilty of this. When my impossible looms large in my life, I lose sight of Who He Is and my circumstances begin to take me down. I know we look at these people and say, how can you not appreciate what Jesus did for you and be forever grateful and yet, that is who we are. We get healed and are shouting one minute, only to realize that we have medical bills to pay now, which seem insurmountable. So our joy becomes a frustrating reality, and we lose sight of the Who He Is because we begin to focus on the new reality of our circumstances. Joseph was given a promise in a dream but it quickly became a nightmare of slavery. Through many years of struggle, that dream was beset by his circumstances as he held onto that dream/promise that God gave him. God was at work behind the scenes although he couldn't see it. Your miracle may come with strings; your rose may come with thorns; your healing may have financial consequences or other realities but it doesn't change Who He Is. Will we be like those who lost sight of the miracle worker and asked Him to leave or will we hold onto the dream through the circumstances knowing Who He Is? It is our choice. How sad that they lost sight of the Who because of the what. Jesus didn't demand to stay. He didn't protest their mistreatment of Him and He will not. He is God. He is undeterred by our circumstances. He is undeterred by our lack of faith. He is working even when we don't see it. This man who was healed wanted to follow Jesus but Jesus told him to stay and minister to others. We never hear anymore about this man other than "As Jesus was getting into the boat, the demon-delivered man begged to go along, but he wouldn't let him. Jesus said, "Go home to your own people. Tell them your story—what the Master did, how he had mercy on you." The man went back and began to preach in the Ten Towns area about what Jesus had done for him. He was the talk of the town."

Mark 5:18-20 MSG

His miracle became his ministry despite others. What will you do with Jesus despite your reality? Will you hold onto the promise through the reality or will you ask Him to leave? Pilate asked them what would they do with this Jesus and they said crucify Him. Despite all the miracles they had seen...what will you do with this Jesus?

Jesus told them, "A prophet has little honor in his hometown, among his relatives, on the streets he played in as a child." Jesus wasn't able to do much of anything there—he laid hands on a few sick people and healed them, that's all. He couldn't get over their stubbornness. He left and made a circuit of the other villages, teaching.

Mark 6: 4-6

Tied Up!

Stubbornness limits faith like a pair of handcuffs on hands. In this chapter of Mark, Jesus is stopping by His hometown area ministering, but because they knew Him as a child, they refused to accept Him as God. What a sad commentary it is that they missed out because of their own stubbornness. Spiritual Immaturity leads to a stubbornness that even God will not deal with in us. He simply walks away and lets us sit in our own mess. Not because He doesn't care or doesn't love us but because we refuse to accept Him as God. We choose to box Him into a corner of our lives as a Deity or Authoritarian that is going to do what He will do, despite us instead of for us. The people He loved the most from His homeland had the same issue. Even though they heard Him and saw the miracles, they could not accept beyond what their eyes could see. And their lack of ability to see Him for Who He is, caused them to miss out on His miracles in their lives. How often are we just like this? We think we know who He is and what He will do based on our experiences so we tie Him up by our lack of faith. We limit His ability to do more for us not because He couldn't bypass us but because He is a gentleman. He is God but He gives us the desires of our heart in accordance with our faith. If we walk in immaturity and doubt then He will not move in our lives because this violates the principles of faith that He set forth under grace. By Faith we are saved, not works, lest anyone should boast. It doesn't matter how good you are or what you do for God if you lack faith that He is who He said He is. I heard a story once of a man named Houdini. He was a very talented magician and his skill was "defying death" by escaping from impossible circumstances. He escaped from straight jackets and leg irons underwater and being buried alive, but was killed by sepsis from a ruptured appendix. He died from blood poisoning six days after his appendix ruptured. He couldn't defy death after all. He only defied what he could control. We are so like this. We think if we control it, then we can manage it, but the truth is that the more we doubt, the more we become entangled. The more we build on ourselves, the more of us there is, the less there is of God and that is where the burdens become too heavy. Those of us who have walked with God a long time are often guilty of putting Him into boxes of limitations because we think we know what He can do; we have seen it but yet our faith hasn't been tested enough to stretch to the unthinkable. Daniel prayed every day three times or more. He was faithful in all things but he still faced the lions' den. He still had to go through the test to come out with the testimony. I don't know what you are going through but I do know that He is Who He says He is. That mountain can be moved. Those chains can be broken. That thing that looks impossible can become the biggest miracle, if you will release it into His hands and truly allow Him to be God. Yes, you may have to walk into a fiery furnace but He will be there with you. Yes, it may seem you are going through it alone and everything you know and everyone you know is turning against you or unable to help you but this is the birthplace of miracles. God of the Impossible only stands out when the Impossible is there. Why? Because we become content with limiting Him to His corner of our lives rather than walking in his full authority and grace. He wants more. He wants to stretch you and use you but you must yield because if you do not, you will break. I think this scripture is one of the saddest in the whole Bible. He couldn't get over their stubbornness...so He left them in it. The KJV says He marveled at their unbelief. Are you tied up in immature unbelief? Have you limited God to a box and a timeline so that he has looked at your unbelief in this same way, shaking His head in grief and walking away? Isn't it time to yield your stubbornness to His strength and get out of His way? There is a miracle on the way but you gotta get out of its way. When the people of Israel were struck by snake bites, Moses erected a staff as God instructed, that they had to look upon to be healed. I wonder how many died in their stubbornness of unbelief rather than going to look upon the pillar as instructed? I wonder how many of us miss Miracles because we are stuck in our stubborn immature behavior of doubt? It is time to disentangle from the world of unbelief and trust in the God of the impossible. Lord, I believe all things are possible.

"I've loved you the way my Father has loved me. Make yourselves at home in my love. If you keep my commands, you'll remain intimately at home in my love. That's what I've done—kept my Father's commands and made myself at home in his love. "I've told you these things for a purpose: that my joy might be your joy, and your joy wholly mature. This is my command: Love one another the way I loved you. This is the very best way to love. Put your life on the line for your friends. You are my friends when you do the things I command you. I'm no longer calling you servants because servants don't understand what their master is thinking and planning. No, I've named you friends because I've let you in on everything I've heard from the Father.

"You didn't choose me, remember; I chose you, and put you in the world to bear fruit, fruit that won't spoil. As fruit bearers, whatever you ask the Father in relation to me, he gives you.

"But remember the root command: Love one another.

John 15: 9-17

Fruit Bearers!

It is that time of year where trees begin to produce fruit and as the flowers change over to fruit, it is important to watch for pests that would destroy the crop. Spiritually we have to do the same. In John, Jesus is telling the disciples about abiding in Him as the vine. He says He has loved us in the same way the Father loves Him. He tells us to make ourselves at home in this love-Godly love. When a guest enters a home, there is a newness to the experience but as they become acquainted with the home, it becomes a place of comfort and assurance. We enjoy staying at VRBOs when we travel because it is easier to relax at a place that has a homey feeling. You don't have to worry about people coming in or dressing for breakfast...it is a roam about as you are kind of thing. That is what God wants for us to feel in His love, not uncertainty but assurance and comfort. Jesus says He no longer calls us servants but friends when we begin to understand the purpose of His love and sacrifice. He says He chose us and put us in this world for the purpose of bearing fruit. The root command though is to Love one another. On my computer, it occasionally has a moment where windows doesn't load properly and the root command screen comes up. When this happened the first time, I had no idea what to do as I was unfamiliar and this was unknown. I consulted with a computer specialist and he instructed me, so now if this occurs, I know the root commands. Jesus tells us that the root command to reset our life on track with Him is Love. He said this for us to understand that He came to give His life out of divine love and that love can live and breathe in us through Him. This is how we obtain the joie de vivre-the joy of life. It is available by abiding or making ourselves at home in His love. Confidence that He is able, willing and will do according to His purpose-which is His love, is the key to joy. Our joy cannot be stolen, it can only be given away. He says Remember, I chose you. The intimacy of being a fruit bearer comes first from the intimacy of knowing His love. Just as a child is birthed from the intimacy of love, the fruit in our lives comes from intimacy in His love. Reboot if you are feeling lost and undone. Come back to His love. Reset your eyes on Him and not the things that draw you away. Refocus on His purpose rather than the storm raging around you. Rehome yourself in His love. Renew your acquaintance then walk into His loving arms. Be a fruit bearer by becoming intimate with Him for He cares for you with an everlasting love.

But now, God's Message,
the God who made you in the first place, Jacob,
the One who got you started, Israel:
"Don't be afraid, I've redeemed you.
I've called your name. You're mine.
When you're in over your head, I'll be there with you.
When you're in rough waters, you will not go down.
When you're between a rock and a hard place,
it won't be a dead end—
Because I am God, your personal God,
The Holy of Israel, your Savior.
I paid a huge price for you:
all of Egypt, with rich Cush and Seba thrown in!
That's how much you mean to me!
That's how much I love you!
I'd sell off the whole world to get you back,
trade the creation just for you.

Isaiah 43: 1-4

Dead End!

I had obviously turned the wrong way, because I reached the sign that said "Dead End", but I was so confused because my GPS kept saying that there was a road ahead. I couldn't see your road. All I could see was the end of the road but my GPS kept telling me there was a road ahead. I decided to keep driving all the way to the sign and sure enough there was a road there. It wasn't much of a road and obviously new, but it was there. I often feel like this in life. I arrive at Dead Ends with no way out but my GPS (God Positioning System) tells me there is a way ahead when I look and it seems there isn't. God was telling His people the same thing here in Isaiah. Don't be afraid to trust because He has redeemed us. When we are in rough waters and in over our heads, He still knows us, and He says we will not go down. He says when we are in between a rock and a hard place, he is our personal God. He paid a huge price for us through the sacrifice of his own son on Calvary, and he is not done with us. He says he would trade creation and sell off the world in order to get us back. I don't know about you, but I have been in some mighty rough waters lately and some days it seems that for sure I am going to drown. Those are the days that I have to cling to his promises as if they are a life raft holding me steady, although precariously in the rough waters. I'll confess that I often get seasick in rough waters. And I will confess that doubt tends to fill my boat as the waters crush over me, over and over, convincing me that this is the end. But then his word speaks to me once again, just as it did today to not be afraid because he has redeemed us. I don't know what you're going through today. It may seem that today is the end for you, but I can promise you that his word says he is your redeemer. He is for you. He said I will be there for you, and he meant every word that he said. I am not a swimmer, but I do love to look at the ocean. A couple of years ago I took my staff to the beach and we decided to take a boat ride. As we're going across the bay, the surf began to get rough, and the boat captain told us to pick up our belongings off the floor, because the water was coming on board. Minutes later water began to rush over the sides of the boat, and my heart began to pound because I knew that we were going to enter here in the ocean, and I didn't swim that well. I knew I had a life vest on so I began to tighten it to make sure that it was on, as I did not know what was ahead. Needless to say, the captain knew what he was doing, and we made it safely to our destination without any more delay or scare. Often in life, though we go through these experiences, or water is rushing on board our life raft, and we're sure that the end is near and we are not gonna make it. That is the time that we need to tighten our life vest, which is the promise that God has given us that he will never leave us. He is the captain of our boat and if we will stay with the boat and tighten our life vest of promises, knowing that He is who he said He is, we will make it safely to our destination. Today, you may feel like you have reached a dead end and your life raft is taking on water. Read His promises and be confident that when you are in over your head, He is there with you.

"The farmer plants the Word. Some people are like the seed that falls on the hardened soil of the road. No sooner do they hear the Word than Satan snatches away what has been planted in them.

"And some are like the seed that lands in the gravel. When they first hear the Word, they respond with great enthusiasm. But there is such shallow soil of character that when the emotions wear off and some difficulty arrives, there is nothing to show for it.

"The seed cast in the weeds represents the ones who hear the kingdom news but are overwhelmed with worries about all the things they have to do and all the things they want to get. The stress strangles what they heard, and nothing comes of it.

"But the seed planted in the good earth represents those who hear the Word, embrace it, and produce a harvest beyond their wildest dreams."

Mark 4: 14-20

Character Soil!

Soil matters! In fact, our "soul soil" determines how well we acclimate and accept the Word that becomes the harvest. In the book of Mark, Jesus has just shared a parable of the farmer with His disciples to help them to understand the role they have in the harvest and the value of soil prep. He likens the Word to the seed and the soil to the soul. He shows us several examples of planting the Word and that wherever it is planted matters. Not only that but that we have the responsibility of prepping our soul soil to take the Word for growth or lack thereof. The first soul He says is hard and as soon as these people hear The Word, Satan snatches it away because they have no acceptance. They haven't tended the soul soil with Living Water and have become hardened to anything God is doing so they miss out on harvest completely. They are starving desert wastelands existing in this world alone-how sad, when Jesus is there waiting. The second comparison is those whose soul soil is granulated like gravel. There are some spots between the rocky places of their soul where a great message or word gets through and they respond enthusiastically but as soon as the emotions wear off, they have such immaturity and shallowness that when hard times arrive, they turn away to their own ways forgetting who He is. They exist only from message to message and emotion to emotion with no depth, just simply shallow character. The third soul soil is that covered in weeds. The seed is cast but the cares of life quickly choke it out because the soul is so busy and concerned with what they have or don't have that they miss out on the Living Water. They only see the haves/have nots rather than eternal things. They are not willing to hoe and toil to develop a richer relationship with Him so they can grow but are consumed with their day to day provisions. They miss out on intimacy and harvest because they are consumed with selfish ambitions. The stresses of life strangle their hope and joy, taking away the harvest. The final illustration is the good earth. This soil has been through some of the previous places but the caretaker decided to invest time in watering so as not to be hardened when planting time came. They took time to pull the rocks and gravel out of their planting area so that they could have depth-they still enjoy the highlights but can withstand the lowlights too. Finally the soul soil was tilled. They saw the potential ahead for hard times and knew that life would bear down on them so they tilled those weeds deep, allowing the cares of life to become fodder and food for their plants rather than an emotional chokehold. They chose to take the impossible situations as places of growth rather than places of loss. They choose through the storms and tough times to keep hoeing, watering and weeding so that when He casts the seed, their soul soil is ready to receive, grow a crop larger than their wildest dreams and harvest it. You see, your character soil is your soul soil. You get to choose. It is an investment. God is laying seeds all the time. He is spreading His seeds abundantly around constantly throughout our days and it is up to us to determine the soul soil. It is our character that we invest in. We can choose to look at the eternal harvest or the shallowness of earthly things. Whatever the seeds of life that God is sowing in us right now, we can determine its growth potential by what we do with our soul soil. Take a measure. Have you grown hardened because you haven't been in the Living Water lately? Time for watering. Have you allowed the gravel of life to become a rocky surface so that you live from emotional high experience to emotional lows? Perhaps it is time to move some gravel out? Have you gotten so caught up in the cares that life brings that you are choking out what God is doing in your life? Maybe it is time to till, hoe and weed your soul soil. His promises are true. His word is life bringing. The seed has all it needs to take root and grow. That mustard seed of faith is just waiting to become a harvest in your life more than you ever imagined but you have to get your soul soil ready to grow the harvest. Lord of the harvest, place your seed in me. I am your servant and I am working on my soul soil. Help me to move the gravel, till the weeds and stay in your overflow so I can be ready for the abundance you are sending my way. Let me keep my eyes in faith and my heart in tune with You.

With many stories like these, he presented his message to them, fitting the stories to their experience and maturity. He was never without a story when he spoke. When he was alone with his disciples, he went over everything, sorting out the tangles, untying the knots.

Awake now, he told the wind to pipe down and said to the sea, "Quiet! Settle down!" The wind ran out of breath; the sea became smooth as glass. Jesus reprimanded the disciples: "Why are you such cowards? Don't you have any faith at all?"

Mark 4: 33-34, 39-40

Untying Knots!

My stomach was knotted up with worry and my heart was pounding. I could see no way to make it through my situation because the storm was raging and the weight of it all was just too much. I turned my car towards my church and walked in on a midweek morning past the people working there straight to the altar so I could crawl in my Father's lap. There I poured out my heart for over an hour. Not because I do not talk to Him daily nor because He doesn't meet me where I am, but because I was in a crisis and knotted up but I knew if I could just crawl in His lap, He would disentangle it all. In these verses in Mark, we see Jesus sharing stories to help people understand His kingdom but then needing to go over it in depth with those closest to Him to disentangle and sort out the tangles and untie the knots. I cannot tell you how many times I get entangled in things that must be sorted out. For years I have been writing a song that God gave me in 2013. Each year, He puts a verse on my heart about what has tied me up or entangled me. These entanglements keep us from seeing the full truth which is why Jesus spends time with us untying the knots we create in our lives. He literally had just sat down explaining faith to His disciples then they got into a boat where He fell asleep. Suddenly a storm arises and they freak out, waking Him up. He calmly says, "Peace, Be still" and the wind lost its breath and the sea became smooth like glass. Then Jesus reprimanded His disciples as He does us. Why in the face of our storms do we so easily lose hope and dive into fear? We know the wind talker and wave walker. He has given us all authority that is His under Heaven. The disciples had the power to command the sea to be still too as Jesus had given them His authority but they walked in lack of faith with fear as their companion when Jesus wasn't awake. Forgive me Lord for my lack of faith and my turning towards fear when You have given me authority to face this mountain of my situation and command it. Allow me to boldly believe and receive the promises you have for me and to walk in confidence that You are working all things out for my good.

Jesus said, "Are you being willfully stupid? Don't you see that what you swallow can't contaminate you? It doesn't enter your heart but your stomach, works its way through the intestines, and is finally flushed." (That took care of dietary quibbling; Jesus was saying that all foods are fit to eat.)

He went on: "It's what comes out of a person that pollutes: obscenities, lusts, thefts, murders, adulteries, greed, depravity, deceptive dealings, carousing, mean looks, slander, arrogance, foolishness—all these are vomit from the heart. There is the source of your pollution."

Mark 7: 18-23

Heart Pollution!

Politics and policies are full of ways to stop pollution of the planet but rarely focus on the true issue of pollution of the heart and soul. In fact, the things that pollute the mind, heart and soul are big business and are highly favored by the government as they are blinded to the truth much as were these politicians of Jesus' time on Earth. Jesus asked His disciples if they were being willfully stupid because He didn't understand how they could possibly miss the reality that pollution of the heart is what makes the soul sick unto death. The politicians of the day, the religious right, were so caught up in the fuss over what to eat and how many times to wash that they missed the point. This often happens to all of us. We get caught up in doing the right thing and missing the thing that is the true source of pollution and sin in our lives. We need hard truth and not platitudes to realize that we are the source of our own mess of heart pollution. Out of the abundance of our heart flows who we are. If we are filled with His Living Water then we flow out from Him but when we fail to fill up constantly, we become stagnant and polluted with life which then pours from our heart out into our world polluting those around us. Jesus lists the source of pollution as the heart and names the pollutants as cursing, lustful desires, stealing, killing, cheating, greed, deprivation, lying, deception, carousing, mean looks, false witnesses, gossip, arrogance, foolishness, etc. These traps and sins are all regurgitated from the heart. When we focus on self, our heart becomes full of polluted mire which then erupts into a volcano of polluted filth out of us, into and onto those around us. Pollution starts at the source and spreads. Jesus says the source is our heart when we focus on the ME instead of HIM. How easy it is to get caught up in this mire. The things we take in to feed on can feed the flesh or the spirit. We choose to fill ourselves with truth or lies. We choose to spend our lifestyle focused on the politics or the pollution when the truth is that we are the source of both. Blaming others is easier than taking a look at our own failures and follies. This is the truth that Jesus was asking His followers if they were willfully stupid about. Do we see or are we being willfully stupid also? Are we ignoring the truths in our own selves? The issues of our lives that pollute our souls are not the things we wrangle with in the day to day from paying the bills to the politics we spend discussing and debating. The issues are all spilling forth from our hearts. If our hearts are focused on Him, then our minds will center on Him and our lives would reflect Him, which would in turn resolve the conflicts of political morass, but when we are focused on self, the deterioration of flesh strives to remake itself and becomes consumed with survival of flesh, resulting in pollution of the heart. If our minds are set on ourselves then all we can see is selfish ambition and desires. We become consumed with our own survival and result in tainted and polluted flesh, which pours out into the lives of those around us in all the ways Jesus described. If we focus on Him, then we pour out Living Water for we are a channel of freshness for Him to pour through. What are we focused on: Ourselves and our wants and desires, which brings about heart pollution and soul death, or are we focusing on Him and filling our lives with His purpose so that He can pour through us in pure life of Living Water?

When they arrived, the Pharisees came out and started in on him, badgering him to prove himself, pushing him up against the wall. Provoked, he said, "Why does this generation clamor for miraculous guarantees? If I have anything to say about it, you'll not get so much as a hint of a guarantee." Meanwhile, the disciples were finding fault with each other because they had forgotten to bring bread. Jesus overheard and said, "Why are you fussing because you forgot bread? Don't you see the point of all this? Don't you get it at all? Remember the five loaves I broke for the five thousand? How many baskets of leftovers did you pick up?"
They said, "Twelve."
"And the seven loaves for the four thousand—how many bags full of leftovers did you get?"
"Seven." He said, "Do you still not get it?"
He then asked, "And you—what are you saying about me? Who am I?"

Mark 8: 11-12, 16-21, 29

Miraculous Hint!

We don't like to compare ourselves to the Pharisees as they are often cast into a negative light in scriptures but too often this is exactly who we are. The Pharisees were not bad people but a ruling class of religious law followers. In fact, many of us are just as legalistic as they were in their time with the "rules" we have created about who is or is not a Christ follower. We judge and force people into boxes. We try to force God's hand by saying, if you are truly God, work out this Or that , show up and do this miraculous thing, perform in this way, etc. Jesus asks, "Why does this generation clamor for miraculous guarantees? If I have anything to say about it, you'll not get so much as a hint of a guarantee." Notice that He didn't say there wasn't a promise of guarantee but He asked why we needed it and said we wouldn't get a hint of one. Why? We like the sure thing...the sure bet...the safe route. Even the disciples who walked with Him and saw Him provide food twice to thousands were freaking out that they forgot lunch and only had one loaf of bread. He asked them, "Do you still not get it?" just as He is asking us. It isn't about the miracle nor the moment. It is about Who He Is! He keeps trying to show us and teach us just as He did His disciples that it isn't about this life, this moment, this trial...there is no need for Him to prove Himself. He IS! He is the Great I AM! His ways are certainly not ours because we are too focused on the external circumstances rather than the truth of who He Is. He asks, "Don't you see the point of all this? Don't you get it at all?" He is trying to say that He is still God in every circumstance rather it be good/bad. He is God today in the sunshine and the same God in the storm. He hasn't changed. His purpose and plan for us didn't change because we are having a bad moment. His plan hasn't changed because our car stops, our work slows down, our AC goes out, etc. He is still God. He still hears and answers but He has no need to prove Himself. He provides because we ask, and we need not so He can prove He is God, but rather because He sees the need before we do. Read back at the miracles of feeding the 5000 and the 4000. Jesus was the one who saw the people hungry and took action. The circumstances were not favorable and the situation looked dire in resource but He saw a need and took the meager resource turning it into an abundance overflowing. He sees our needs before we think to ask. He provides a way before us. His path isn't about making the way easy to walk, see and understand but rather teaching us the way of trusting that He is enough. Recently I went up in an airplane with my son. I knew nothing about what He was doing to navigate nor fly the plane but I trusted that he did and he got us safely there and back. Why is it so easy for us to trust that a piece of metal filled with people and an engine can get up into the air, transport us hundreds of miles safely and land but we cannot trust God's timely provisions? When we go to sit in a chair, we trust the chair to hold us based on evidence that other chairs have held us. We use evidence of reliability. God has proven time and time again to be reliable and provides, so why do we still not "get it"? Instead we bicker over the loaf rather than just handing it to Him and saying, I messed up and I need you to be my provider. Here is my loaf, my circumstances, my car, my finances, my AC, my kid, my "whatever", do with it what you will. Then allow Him to be God. He is God. He doesn't need our stamp of approval so no hints. No cheating allowed. Only trusting that He who said He is, is who He said He was. He asks, "Who Do You say I Am?" Peter answered Him in truth but the question is ours to answer daily. Who is He? He is the same God and He lives in us. That is the miraculous hint. No guarantee needed. Our lives alone are a daily walking miracle. That is our miracle. Embrace it and begin to walk in it. The same God that raised the dead, lives in us.

But what happens when we live God's way? He brings gifts into our lives, much the same way that fruit appears in an orchard–things like affection for others, exuberance about life, serenity. We develop a willingness to stick with things, a sense of compassion in the heart, and a conviction that a basic holiness permeates things and people. We find ourselves involved in loyal commitments, not needing to force our way in life, able to marshal and direct our energies wisely.

Legalism is helpless in bringing this about; it only gets in the way. Among those who belong to Christ, everything connected with getting our own way and mindlessly responding to what everyone else calls necessities is killed off for good–crucified.

Galatians 5: 22-24

Directed Energy!

As I sat with the matriarch of our family discussing everything and nothing, the gifts of God's goodness flowed between us like eating fruit in an orchard. We toured her lovely home and reflected on the ebbs and flow of life realizing that lifestyle isn't what matters but His love does. I watched her ways and heard her wisdom, saw her love, affection and compassion as she went about her day from the small motions to the simple convictions. When we live God's way, it isn't always easy, but it is full of adventure and energy. He produces the fruit in our lives that nurtures others and draws them to us. Being stuck in rules and manners makes us dependent on law but being a servant of Christ brings about a selfless good. As I moved about precariously due to my back bothering me, I began to focus on other things around me. The beauty of His creation, the restoration of life to my beautiful youngest aunt after devastating loss, and the tranquility of His goodness in the man of grace God had brought in my aunt's life settled in my spirit. These are His gifts to us. As we drove through an orchard of grapevines and fruit, we saw the owner had put netting around the fruit to protect it from all the pests and birds. She had provided the stability and support for the vines to grow and the water lines to give constant nourishment as well as the protection for the fruit to remain untouched until the time came for the harvesting. I know that when the time of harvest comes, those grapes will be crushed and pressed to produce wine. That gardener nourishes them now for a future harvest and purpose just like God gives us times of growing, producing and harvesting which many times requires crushing and pressing to get the things He wants from us. When we truly live God's way, He brings gifts into our lives like fruit in an orchard but these do not come without consequences and trial. The fruit of love comes through adversity and loss so we understand the value. The fruit of patience comes through trials so we can see His goodness in the pressing. The fruit of peace and serenity comes through the trusting, during the storms of life. The exuberance of life, goodness, meekness, self control, grit, comes by sticking with it in the hard times. Compassion and kindness, holiness, conviction, and loyalty all come through the teachings of a life lived in Him. There is no need to push ourselves forward or try being more than what we are for He is our source and provider. I have watched these women from afar. I have seen their battles and their scars which have produced an uncanny beauty as they have ripened. Necessity or what we feel we must have is sacrificed in the making. When God remakes us in His image, we are pressed into a fine wine or fresh juice of His making. Not a sour mash or an alcoholic mess but a beautiful substance for His glory. This isn't a commentary on drinking or alcohol. This is a truth of His developing us into the fruit of His orchard. We are the branches and He is the Vine. We are the fruit producers and He is the gardener. We are the clay and He is the potter. Whatever type of illustration you need, the truth remains. We are His. When we yield into His keeping all our ways, He brings good things, gifts and fruit and development and beauty into our lives. Lord, I am so grateful for you. I am blessed every morning by Your faithfulness to me throughout this journey called life. Help me to be all You desire me to be as You make a fine fruit juice or wine of me through the crushing and pressing. Help me to let go of the trappings of what I think life should be so I can be fully immersed in what You have for me to do. I want to be used by You and be as You are.

Soak me in your laundry and I'll come out clean,
scrub me and I'll have a snow-white life.
Tune me in to foot-tapping songs,
set these once-broken bones to dancing.
Don't look too close for blemishes,
give me a clean bill of health.
God, make a fresh start in me,
shape a Genesis week from the chaos of my life.
Don't throw me out with the trash,
or fail to breathe holiness in me.
Bring me back from gray exile,
put a fresh wind in my sails!
Give me a job teaching rebels your ways
so the lost can find their way home.
Commute my death sentence, God, my salvation
God, and I'll sing anthems to your life-giving
ways. Unbutton my lips, dear God;
I'll let loose with your praise.

Psalms 51: 7-15

Soaked Clean!

As with all fads, people are now putting their sheets/towels into the bathtubs and posting pictures of the dirty water after they have soaked the laundry. There is a difference in a deep water soaking and a light water washing. It is the reason I have a deep water cycle with an agitator still in my washing machine. A fresh start requires a good soaking but also a look for blemishes to identify the places of brokenness and tears. When laundry is dirty, it has a foul stench that spreads to the clothes around it. When someone has a stinky attitude, it also spreads and can contaminate everything around it with the foulness. David prayed for God to tune him into foot tapping songs and set the broken bones to dancing. He knew that joy is found in God and not our circumstances. As he prayed, he asked God to give him a fresh beginning even though he felt like he was in gray exile. Nowadays we are quick to throw away rather than mend. I see this happen with everything from mismatched socks to marriages. If there is a tear in the marriage sheet, rather than darn it or attempt repairing, we are quick to label it unhealthy and toss it away. Our value of individuals and life is not what it once was. The newness has faded and we have become jaded to what God is doing. We get stuck in our own stench so that we refuse to see Him working and we become so used to our own ways that we fail to yield to Him. In this passage, David realized his follies and repented asking for a fresh start. He begged not to be thrown out in the garbage or left without God's breath in his life to direct him. He understood the value of God's hand upon his life. God, unbutton my lips, he prayed, so I can sing your praises. A fresh wind does wonders for the clean laundry. It invites the fragrance of outdoors and dries the items naturally. When we get a fresh start or new wind, it is easy for others who haven't to taint us and ruin what God is trying to do in us, especially if they are not yielding. Sometimes we have no choice about association because they are family or close connections. I want to soak in His presence so deeply and steep His goodness into every fiber of my being then be cleansed of all the negativity so that I can dry in the Sonshine of His love and take in all He has for me. This is the only way that I can go about with songs of praise instead of the oh me, oh mys. When we steep in our own stench, it soaks into us so deeply that others around us want to avoid us as our negativity becomes offensive and off putting. We become so stinky in our attitudes towards God and everything and everyone that our very presence taints those around us. You don't put dirty clothes with clean because the dirty will taint the clean. When dirty soiled mindsets come at you, especially after a recent cleansing, that is when you must begin to steep in his presence through song and getting into His presence for only He can change the hearts of men. Dirty rotten, stinky attitudes towards God's goodness and provisions are not going to bring cleanness nor lightness. They will only weigh you down. Praises break down prison walls. The prison of your mind filled with negativity and "stinking thinking" will not be cleared by adding more muck and more attitudinal negativity. The only way to get free from the prison of your mind and see your circumstances as an adventure through the Red Sea is by breaking down those prison walls with praise and quoting His promises over the negative situations. Sitting in the muck, adding to the stench with stinking words and perspective only makes the hole you are in deeper and wider and more impossible. You have the ability to praise no matter your circumstances. Get out into the sunshine and begin to reflect on His goodness instead of sitting in the darkness of your mind. The gray exile of oppression is real. The way out is praise. Fresh wind comes with testifying to His goodness through it all. Yes, your situation may look impossible but He is still the God of possibility in the impossible. Tell Him about it. Unbutton your lips and begin to praise. Prison walls come down with praise.

Jesus said, "You're way off base, and here's why: One, you don't know what God said; two, you don't know how God works. After the dead are raised up, we're past the marriage business. As it is with angels now, all our ecstasies and intimacies then will be with God. And regarding the dead, whether or not they are raised, don't you ever read the Bible? How God at the bush said to Moses, 'I am—not was—the God of Abraham, the God of Isaac, and the God of Jacob'? The living God is God of the living, not the dead. You're way, way off base."

Mark 12: 24-27

Off Base!

I Am, not I was! What a powerful statement. The living God is God of the living and all our ecstasies and intimacies will be with God. What powerful promises He has given us. As Jesus admonished these people for their feeble minds of thought, I felt His tug to listen and read it again. The Living God of intimate knowledge of us says we're way off base when we are caught up in the transfer of this carnal life to that of eternity. We don't have His mindset. We get caught up in minuscule wanderings. In this case, they were asking whose wife a woman was if she was married to brothers who had died-all I thought about was, poor woman. Our carnal mindset even when redeemed, is only able to picture or plan so much as far as eternity because we are finite. It is nice to picture new bodies without the flaws and foibles but our mindset even in spirit is limited to what we can grasp. Bases are loaded, Jesus went to bat, He hit a home run that opened all of Heaven to us to run into Home and yet..., many cannot see, will not run, limit themselves to the next base of life only. His admonition is we don't know what God said and we don't know how God works. He isn't limited to this plane, this event, the circumstances or by our situations. He is the I AM, not the I was. The same God who raised people from the grave lives in us. That same power rests in us. We have His authority and our circumstances are no match for Him and His authority but it does take us being willing to see. God is not limited by our abilities nor our faith or lack thereof but He chooses to abide in us. He chooses to use our circumstances to refine us into His image. Why do we choose so often to fight in carnal warfare instead of spiritual? We know the battles of this world are often spiritual and not fleshly, so why do we get down into the weeds fighting when God has a weed-eater that can mow it all down with a single word? When playing baseball, the off base time is the time of danger because that is the time when you can be caught out, tagged and miss out on the run. Stealing a base means risking this and requires faith in your own abilities to make it, but in a home run, the ball is so far gone that every player has the opportunity to run home. Despite this, some struggle in fear and have to be egged on by the fans or bystanders or other players to overcome so they can make it. We are called to do that. We are called to push others towards the mark of high calling and eternal hope. We are called to encourage one another, push one another to the next place of running the bases home. It is easy to fatigue in the game of life, get stuck or discouraged. The enemy of our soul even tries using every means possible to fake us out by pretending he has the ball and can get us out, but the truth is, the home run is so far gone that he is powerless and he knows it so he lies and feints pretending. Our circumstances may seem tough and fear may truly beset us but the Living God says He is the I Am, not the I was. Satan wants to distract us into staying on the base we are on because he knows the home run has been cast. Fear, death, hell and the grave have all been conquered by the home run Jesus hit at Calvary. Do not let fear keep you on first base when the home run has been hit. Get back to running the bases as the conquering team. Know what God said and know how God works by becoming intimate with Him in His word and prayer and praise. No mountain is bigger than He is and He has already overcome it. Get out of the weeds and start running home.

But how can people call for help if they don't know who to trust? And how can they know who to trust if they haven't heard of the One who can be trusted? And how can they hear if nobody tells them? And how is anyone going to tell them, unless someone is sent to do it? That's why Scripture exclaims,
A sight to take your breath away!
Grand processions of people
telling all the good things of God!
But not everybody is ready for this, ready to see and hear and act. Isaiah asked what we all ask at one time or another: "Does anyone care, God? Is anyone listening and believing a word of it?" The point is: Before you trust, you have to listen. But unless Christ's Word is preached, there's nothing to listen to.

Mark 10: 14-17

See, Hear, Act!

Trust is such a precarious thing in our current culture. Paul is exhorting the church in Romans to be doers and tellers of the Words of Life so others can hear, see and act. Not everyone is ready for that. Some have to watch and trust for a while because they have been burned or betrayed. Sending people out to tell others about Jesus, missionaries and ministers and youth groups, etc. must first minister to the felt needs in order to build trust that allows them to not only hear but to listen. You can hear and not listen. Listening involves tuning the heart and mind towards that being said so you can measure its veracity and value. In today's society, the script has been flipped to guilty until proven innocent and anyone who is unhappy can blast you online, contact people you know and love, ruining reputation and tearing down what has been built for years. Recently, as a victim of scam and fraud, I have felt this vicious attack and it is horrible. It undermines your trust in yourself and others and when your spirit cries out without answer, your heart fails you in trusting God. These are the times to rest in His promises and know He is in control. Sometimes when things are especially hard, I feel like screaming "Does anyone care, God? Is anyone listening or believing a word of the promises?" His word is true. He says that anything that can be shaken will be shaken in the last days. We need to prepare our hearts and minds. Be alert because the devil is going about as a roaring lion seeking to devour us. Trust comes from hearing and listening to the Word of God and enables us to stand when the Earthquakes riot our lives. How can others know the One who can be trusted unless they first learn of Him. Our trials are not for our sake alone but to help others stand when the impossible shakes their world. What are we to do? Be a part of the Grand Procession of People telling all the good things of God! Isaiah was right, we all question God and whether anyone cares, at one time or another in our lives, but the knowing in the midst of the storm is the key. Take time to listen to His sweet voice because to trust you must first listen. Maybe you are being sent in a way you never expected to have to go. Trust Him.

So let's not allow ourselves to get fatigued doing good. At the right time we will harvest a good crop if we don't give up, or quit. Right now, therefore, every time we get the chance, let us work for the benefit of all, starting with the people closest to us in the community of faith.

Galatians 6: 9-10

Bone Weary!

Fatigued. Just tired of the struggle. Ready to quit. Whether it is marriage or job or situational stress or life, we all get bone weary. Doing good for others and treating them kindly is hard when tiredness has sapped one's energy and drive. In Hebrews, we are instructed to not allow ourselves to get fatigued doing good. I will say I have always concentrated on the second line, that we will harvest a good crop if we don't give up or quit but somehow missed the "not allow". This is likely due to the fact that promises are more enjoyable when they don't have strings attached. As we sat discussing our memories of certain things, it was apparent that our perception was different from one person to the other. What one person perceived as one thing was really another. A parent disciplining or saving the child from danger can be misunderstood by the child to be punishment. Change in a positive way that we agree with is fun and exciting but when change comes without our willing participation, it seems like an attack. Sticking to doing good is only a part of the hardest thing...the keep going is the biggest part. A social definition of insanity is doing the same thing over and over expecting a different result but the reality is that doing the same thing over and over creates learning and often leads to innovation. Your days may seem monotonous and you may feel stuck but God is constantly at work in our circumstances. Keep going in the good. Do not give up on God. As I look across the water in this beautiful nature, it seems placid and unchanging but then as I look closer, I see a rapid current. Change is happening even as it seems to not be happening. Some of that change is good and some hard. Hard changes are not usually comfortable nor easy. Sometimes we have to get bone weary in the place we are in so we are willing to change. Sometimes the uncertainty can be super scary and unstable feeling, but even that can be God directing. The impossible can be a platform to greatness if we "allow ourselves" to continue in His ways despite our current circumstances. If we remember to "not allow" ourselves to give up or get tired in the midst of the doing. I think of all the hard workers in the church that I know who push through despite their circumstances. I don't understand His plans and ways, but I know that trusting in Him despite and continuing forward in the "doing good" is the key to opening His perfect will for us. There is a story of a man seeing a boy throwing seashells back into the sea. An older man walked up to him and asked what he was doing. He said I am throwing these crabs in shells back into the water to live. The man looked around and saw hundreds of thousands of shells. He told the boy what you are doing doesn't matter, you will never be able to do it and save them. The boy calmly bent over and threw another one, and calmly responded, "it might not matter to all but it mattered to that one". This is the truth. The circumstances we are in may seem huge and the people around us may have become additional naysayers just like the people surrounding Job but just like this boy, Job knew that God was working despite what it looked like. Do not let your circumstances dictate your destiny. God is bigger than these situations and He is working on our behalf. Don't give up or quit. Keep working for the good crop. Keep pulling those weeds, hoeing the hard ground, planting and watering for the good harvest is coming.

Worry weighs us down; a cheerful word picks us up.
A good person survives misfortune, but a wicked life invites disaster.

Proverbs 12:25-26

Worry Weight!

The waves of worry beat at me from every side from boss to daughter, to mother to wife and the list goes on. Our bodies are not created to bear the weight of worry because we are created in God's image and He doesn't worry. He tells us repeatedly not to worry but to cast all our cares on Him and that worry just weighs us down. Yet, we as humans think we know better so we worry. Worry is the result of a lack of trust. We do not like to admit that but the truth is that we are curious and unsettled in our natures. God created us with a desire to commune with Him-a God sized hole only He can fill. When we are not content and full of Him, the empty spot begins to fill with worry. The less of Him, the more we worry and vice versa. Worry weighs us down, keeping us from riding the waves of love. It can be a weight dragging us to the depths causing us to drown in the overwhelming waves of life rather than relaxing in the tides of His love. So, how do we combat worry when it is such a natural emotion to we humans? We pray, then trust, then speak, then act. The prayer of a righteous person avails much and God's promise says no good thing will be withheld from those who walk uprightly. We pray and begin to walk in His promises even when we feel tied down and water is rising. Then the trust/faith part comes. This is the toughest part and requires strict discipline. Faith is a test and an asset of trust. It is the activation but oh it can be so hard. Weighed down and knotted up by worry, the tide rising around us and no answers of rescue in sight. This letting go place is the place of true trust. It is the place where we give it all over to God and we wait to see what He will do. It is a place of quiet from Him and storms all around. It is a scary and tumultuous place. It is the meeting place with God Himself. It is a place of promise and potential. The promise is that good people survive misfortunes. Be of good cheer for God has overcome.

But me, I'm not giving up.
I'm sticking around to see what God will do.
I'm waiting for God to make things right.
I'm counting on God to listen to me.
Spreading Your Wings
Don't, enemy, crow over me.
I'm down, but I'm not out.
I'm sitting in the dark right now,
but God is my light.
I can take God's punishing rage.
I deserve it—I sinned.
But it's not forever. He's on my side
and is going to get me out of this.
He'll turn on the lights and show me his ways.
I'll see the whole picture and how right he is.
And my enemy will see it, too,
and be discredited—yes, disgraced!
This enemy who kept taunting,
"So where is this God of yours?"
I'm going to see it with these, my own eyes—
my enemy disgraced, trash in the gutter.

Micah 7: 7-10

Counting On!

I am not sure there is anything more disheartening than counting on something or someone that falls through or fails whether it be person or situation. Not only is it painful but it is easily a joy stealer. Putting our emotions on the line with people and promises leads to disappointment, but never investing or risking leads to never gaining anything. In this chapter of Micah, he states that he isn't giving up, he's sticking it out to see what God will do. I'm waiting for God to listen to me and make things right. I'm down but I'm not out. I'm sitting in the dark but God is my light. I remember when my son was little and he got into trouble. I heard him in his room talking to himself. He said, "I did it and she is mad right now, but she loves me". He was affirming his own knowledge that he had made a mistake that got him into trouble but that I still loved him despite it all. I have to do this sometimes with God in my situations. I have to affirm myself in Him stating what I know to be true even though it doesn't feel true. I have to remember that my circumstances are not forever whether it be pain, sickness or struggle. I have to confess to myself that He is still on my side and will get me out of this even though I feel alone. I have to remember that I am only seeing a little in this darkness and He will turn on His light so all will be made right. We are all sinners and we all make mistakes but that is when the miracle of God's love shines brightest.

The truth is, it is often hard to see in the dark. The dark places sap our strength, our happiness, and often they take away our ability to see hope. That's why we must have an internal strength in the word of God so that in these very dark and trying places we can "trust his word and know that no matter what our situation is, he will still turn it into something good". I do not know where you are today, and I do not know your situation. But I do know that I have been in some very dark and trying situations, and even as I write this, I am in the hardest battle in my entire life. Micah, the prophet, wrote these words, while he was going through some very big struggles. The people around us may say, "So where is this God of yours?" They may mock and deride and put down, but He will show up and he will put our enemies under our feet and make things right even if it doesn't look like we think it will. He is on our side and He will show up. When you cannot count on anyone else, and you cannot count on anything else, you can count on God.

"And watch out! They're going to drag you into court. And then it will go from bad to worse, dog-eat-dog, everyone at your throat because you carry my name. You're placed there as sentinels to truth. The Message has to be preached all across the world. "When they bring you, betrayed, into court, don't worry about what you'll say. When the time comes, say what's on your heart—the Holy Spirit will make his witness in and through you.
"It's going to be brother killing brother, father killing child, children killing parents. There's no telling who will hate you because of me.

Mark 13: 9-13

Staying Power!

Letting go is so much easier than staying and continuing when it is hard. This is true for marriage, career and life as well as a spiritual principle. Satan is on a warpath like never before attacking everyone I know as he knows his time is very short. He read God's word because he knows God is God and he will never measure up but oh that irritates him. God is in control. We are placed here as truth speakers who hold the name of God above all circumstances. The attacks on us from personal to financial, to health, to mental, to emotional are growing as time draws to a close. What we must remember is that we are the truth sentinels. Lies abound as the evil grows and the love of many grows cold to what God has because they cannot get their own way. They want to enjoy the season of sin while also speaking the name of God and this is exactly what happened throughout scripture. We cannot serve two masters. We cannot love God and put Him first while catering to the whims and fancies of men. Either we love God fully and hate the ways of the world that are based on carnality or we do not truly love God. Harsh truth: you cannot embrace the rainbow of God's promise then equate it to a life of lust and sin. God's not duplicitous. His love is pure. If we carry a light into darkness, then discard the light for the darkness, what was the point? Light and darkness do not coexist. Light dispels darkness. God hates sin. He despises the fraud of iniquity and things like "little white lies", because there is no such thing. Sin is sin. We are either truth seekers and sentinels or liars. I am not saying we do not make mistakes because we absolutely do. I am not saying we are unforgiven because God's grace is infinite. What I am saying is that we are in the last days when the divide of truth will be the sword that separates. We will face hard times, challenges and even people who betray us, lie about us and more. Not too long ago, I was standing in a grocery line behind two women and I heard them discussing me as if we were friends. One woman told the other that I had just gotten divorced (news to me as it hadn't happened) and that my business was closing (again, a lie). She droned on about how close we were as friends although I had never met her and she didn't even say my name correctly. As they were getting ready to leave, I said, excuse me, may I give you my business card and introduce myself? Shock and stammering ensued. I didn't need to argue or defend myself. I just introduced the truth and it cut the lies down swiftly. Many times lately as I have walked through trials, I remember that moment when I felt betrayed and horrified but God told me to hold my tongue until He revealed the timing. That vindication by truth was powerful and not wicked or evil. I didn't have to argue, persuade or prove. I just needed to stand in truth. Whatever we go through in our lives, God's truth is without measure. If we stand in His truth that He is who he says He is, then we can stand through it all knowing that no matter what happens, He wins. Don't let life take the truth away. Don't stand in your truth as the world dictates because that is a place of shifting sands and danger. Walk instead in God's truth. Greater is He that is in us than he that is of this world. Watch out! Stay with His truth and we will be saved.

Jesus told them, "You're all going to feel that your world is falling apart and that it's my fault. There's a Scripture that says,
I will strike the shepherd;
The sheep will scatter.
"But after I am raised up, I will go ahead of you, leading the way to Galilee."
Going a little ahead, he fell to the ground and prayed for a way out: "Papa, Father, you can—can't you?—get me out of this. Take this cup away from me. But please, not what I want—what do you want?"

Mark 14: 27-28, 35-36

Falling Apart!

I tried to pick it up but it crumbled in my hands. This thing of beauty that I admired had quickly become a mess. It looked so pretty and delicate sitting there that I didn't realize it was but a pile that upon my touch was nothing more than grains of sand. When our world that we have spent much time and effort investing in, comes crashing down around us, it is so easy to blame God. We blame Him for allowing it, for not intervening and even for not moving as He promised. We blame Him for blessing others and not us, for forgetting who we are, for not being faithful as He promised and yet, He told us this would happen. Jesus knew the way ahead as He was God but He also knew His flesh was human. He prayed. He entered a dark place and asked his disciples to pray with Him but the fatigue of night and a meal was upon them and they fell asleep. Jesus suffered in agony, all alone, praying and begging God to remove this cup of iniquity from Him but ultimately He submitted to the will of God. The battle of Calvary happened in the Garden of Gethsemane. Yes, He could've stopped it right there. In fact, that is the battle we all face. It is the battle of will. The beauty of that sculpture was created by God in nature but destroyed by my hand. I saw the beauty and couldn't resist touching it, possessing it. My hand was the thing that caused the destruction of what He had created. Jesus told His disciples and through them, us, that we would feel like our world was falling apart and that it is God's fault. He knew we would reach a place of putting our hand in it, destroying His creation and blaming Him. He knew and prepared a way out in advance. He prepared and set the example of prayer through the trial and victory in prayer before the verdict. In victory, the outcome of this world doesn't matter. In victory, the flesh gives way to the spirit and the truth is revealed. The darkest hours that plague the body and mind are those just before dawn. These are the hours where prayer creates vision beyond our will so that we can yield to the will of the Father. There are no promises that we will not have hard times. In fact, He said in this world we will have trials but we are to be of good cheer despite these because He has overcome the world. It may look like our world is falling apart by the standards of man but God has already won and in this place of our Gethsemane, we can conquer through His victory over all in prayer. Papa Father, I know You can get me out of these situations and difficulties, but please do not do what I want, but what You want. I am willing to go where You want me to go and take my hand away from what You are doing. My world is falling apart Lord, but I trust You. I'll do what You put before me to do. I cannot see the way ahead as it is dark and scary but I trust You. I will say what You want me to say and be what You want me to be. In this time of dark before the dawn, I pray Your will not mine. Please go before me and make my path straight so I will not wander off but will stay where You direct me. Not my will but Yours be done in these situations of my life.

By entering through faith into what God has always wanted to do for us—set us right with him, make us fit for him—we have it all together with God because of our Master Jesus. And that's not all: We throw open our doors to God and discover at the same moment that he has already thrown open his door to us. We find ourselves standing where we always hoped we might stand—out in the wide open spaces of God's grace and glory, standing tall and shouting our praise.

There's more to come: We continue to shout our praise even when we're hemmed in with troubles, because we know how troubles can develop passionate patience in us, and how that patience in turn forges the tempered steel of virtue, keeping us alert for whatever God will do next. In alert expectancy such as this, we're never left feeling shortchanged. Quite the contrary—we can't round up enough containers to hold everything God generously pours into our lives through the Holy Spirit!

Romans 5:1-5

Alert Expectancy!

In the Old Testament of scripture, there is a story of a woman who needed money to protect her children from being sold into slavery because their father had died leaving a large debt owed. The prophet asks the woman what she has in her possession and she says only a little oil. The prophet told her to gather as many vessels as she could find, even borrowing them, then go into her home and begin pouring oil into the vessels. After they were filled, she was told to sell them to repay the debt. The oil never ran out. The miracle of provision didn't come in an instant; it came through faithfulness of walking it out through passionate patience. She had the opportunity to make more or less by the amount of investment of effort she put in. She had to collect jars and borrow jars. I imagine people thought her a little desperate, perhaps even a little lost and confused as she went around borrowing jars. By entering through faith into what God through the prophet said He wanted to do for her, she rounded up containers to hold what God generously poured into that singular vessel. We are that singular vessel. God is pouring into us but we are charged with rounding up containers to hold the oil of God that He is pouring. The amount of what we have looks bleak and not enough. The world around us looks at us saying it isn't enough, telling us we need to quit, give up, throw in the towel but God is telling us to round up vessels for He is doing a new thing. We have a choice. We can throw open the doors of faith to walk into wide open spaces of God's provision and see that He is already meeting our needs before we ask or think or we can protect ourselves and the little we possess by harboring it. Paul said to continue to shout praises even while hemmed in with troubles because this develops passionate patience which becomes tempered steel. I can just imagine that moment when she began to pour, the sense of awe and expectation growing as first one vessel then another was filled from that tiny, unending source of oil. God desires to fill us as the vessel that has no end to His anointing but we must ready the vessels. We must prepare the way. We must go out and seek the vessels to be filled. Each of us has a marketplace of ministry that God has given us to pour His anointed love, joy and truth into lives. We must begin to walk in the truth of who He is as the source of the anointing oil that is never quenched. The truth is that when this woman in need stopped pouring, the oil stopped flowing. When we stop pouring into others, our source becomes clogged. If we keep pouring out praise and joy and love, through our troubles then the hand of God continues to stay active in us. I imagine her hands got tired, her back got sore, her legs and arms ached but she kept pouring until all the vessels she had were filled. We may feel used up, tired and of no use anymore but God says He is still pouring as long as we are willing to be the vessel. No matter what the circumstances from pain to loss, He is not finished with us. The season of life may look as different in size and shape as the vessels this lady filled but just know that whatever is before you is the vessel He wants you to fill. The vessel may look ugly or distorted. It may be difficult to maneuver and manage but He has provided that vessel for you to pour into through your troubles. Allow God to use you as a vessel of His anointing to be poured into all you meet. Sure she was scared, who wouldn't be with the threat of her children being sold into slavery for a debt. She didn't let fear keep her still. It motivated her to dig deeper and go get more vessels. God is pouring out His anointing oil of His spirit through us as His vessels. Start pouring out into the lives around you and watch what He will do. Don't stop pouring because His love is unending. Walk into your day with alert expectancy instead of feeling short changed. Round up containers of life to pour into today.

Still later, as the Eleven were eating supper, he appeared and took them to task most severely for their stubborn unbelief, refusing to believe those who had seen him raised up. Then he said, "Go into the world. Go everywhere and announce the Message of God's good news to one and all. Whoever believes and is baptized is saved; whoever refuses to believe is damned.

Mark 16: 14-16

Stubborn Unbelief!

What is a miracle? What is a blessing? Both are based on belief. After Jesus was raised from the dead, the disciples were told by several people that they had seen Him but yet, though they had walked with Him and seen the miracles and heard Him say this very thing, they did not believe. Belief is a choice despite the circumstances. Faith is the substance of things hoped for and the evidence of things unseen. When Jesus appeared to them at supper, He rebuked them for their stubborn unbelief. How much we are just like these disciples in our lives! Each day, as we awake, we experience miracles but yet we walk as if the world has the authority and not Him. The very existence of us living on this planet is a miracle of gravity and yet, we trust the science and not the God who placed the planet we live on in space. Recently I sat down into a chair, trusting it because each chair I have sat in holds me. This chair was not put together properly and as soon as I sat in it, it collapsed. I didn't blame the chair but instead looked for the issue that caused the collapse to understand why it failed so it might be corrected. We are so quick to doubt and trust the Creator instead of looking into our own hearts and minds to see what is causing the collapse of our "chair" that has failed us. We easily give up in despair when things don't go as we would like instead of looking to God and trusting His hand. Our stubborn unbelieving will puts us at odds with who He is. He has charged us with believing that He is who He says He is and going into our marketplace of ministry with our head held high delivering this good news that He is the way, truth and life. The belief is the action that spurs the opening of the doors of life. The chair I had sat in had a construction issue that made it faulty and until it was corrected, it was not stable. Many times our lives are built on things that have failures and flaws which create unstable situations. These can be people, careers, lifestyles, etc. but it is our role to examine them and align them to the truth. We cannot correct our ways unless we are first willing to examine why. We must be willing to receive corrections and recognize our failures so we can align once again to His glory. The belief in who He is opens the doors to miracles and blessings in our lives but if we stubbornly refuse to believe what He says and who He is, then we fall into the category of those who refuse to believe and are damned. Belief is unwavering conviction. Belief is knowing despite what things look like or feel like. Belief is looking through His vision instead of carnal eyesight. Belief is expectation. Belief is understanding that all things are possible only through Him. Most of us believe in technology because we have seen it work. We send a text by typing it on a smartphone and we believe when we hit send that it arrives to that other device through the air. Why is it so easy to believe that our words travel through unseen spaces to another device but so difficult to believe that God, who created all things, including the air we breathe, can intervene in our hard places? Do we want to be taken to task most severely by God for our unbelief? We have scriptures and evidence that He is who He says He is. We have blessings and have seen miracles in our lives. Isn't it time we begin to trust and give up our stubborn unbelief so we can be effective tools in His kingdom? We may get down and feel like God has forgotten us when we are faced with circumstances we cannot seem to get through. It may seem that there is no way out and we are going under but the truth is that He has proven time and again that He will take care of us. We only have to let go of our stubborn unbelief and trust His nail scarred hands. He will make a way where there seems to be no way! He will do it again!

But the angel said, "I am Gabriel, the sentinel of God, sent especially to bring you this glad news. But because you won't believe me, you'll be unable to say a word until the day of your son's birth. Every word I've spoken to you will come true on time–God's time."

"And did you know that your cousin Elizabeth conceived a son, old as she is? Everyone called her barren, and here she is six months pregnant! Nothing, you see, is impossible with God."

And Mary said,
Yes, I see it all now:
I'm the Lord's maid, ready to serve.
Let it be with me
just as you say.
Then the angel left her.

Luke 1: 19-20, 36-38

Heart Contrast!

Acceptance of certain news or announcements can be taken in different ways. An unexpected pregnancy is a joy but often incites fear of the unknown just as other unexpected circumstances from illnesses such as cancer to financial stressors to emotional upheavals. How we approach these varies but the way we approach them matters. Looking in Luke, we see the contrast of acceptance of the unexpected news of pregnancy. Zechariah and Elizabeth had served God faithfully all their lives and had prayed for a child diligently but it appeared their prayers had gone unanswered. Neither gave up serving God but Zechariah harbored doubt in his heart about God though he was a priest. This doubt and unbelief lay in his heart and when an angel appeared to him to announce that his elderly wife was going to have a child, he was skeptical as he had given up on God doing this. He did not believe the Angel Gabriel and asks how it can be since they are old. The Angel senses the unbelief and Zechariah was struck mute until his son was born-a period of a year or so. Gabriel said, "every word I've spoken to you will come true on time-God's time". This is the pinnacle factor. God's timing. The timing was the reason why the doubt or unbelief had grown in Zechariah's heart. Zechariah had grown weary of waiting on God and allowed doubt to gain footing in his heart growing into unbelief. The contrast of acceptance of news is evident in Mary. Only a few months after visiting Zechariah, the Angel Gabriel visits Mary. Mary is a young maiden engaged to be married to Joseph. A strange man-this angel--appears in her bedchamber startling her. He makes the announcement that she will give birth to the son of God and Mary asks how. The angel explains and gives evidence then Mary responds, "Let it be with me just as you say." Both people questioned the news delivered by Gabriel. Both wondered how it could happen as it seemed impossible. The difference was the heart posture. Mary's heart was open and willing despite it being a very awkward situation which would result in lots of problems and questions. Zechariah doubted God's ability and questioned from a place of unbelief while Mary openly trusted and accepted despite the insurmountable issues ahead. Zechariah was much older, had served God all his life, was intimately involved in leading the people in worship of God and knew the scripture, yet he had allowed a place of doubt to create a place of unbelief in his heart, blocking him from seeing the impossible as possible through God. Our heart posture matters! God's will was happening either way in His time. Mary's acceptance of it allowed her to experience a full intimacy with God beyond what the priest of God had because of her heart posture. Heart posture is correctable with time, prayer and purpose. We must determine to capture any lingering thoughts of doubt or fear as they appear in our lives. We must speak God's word and promises over these. We must like Mary be ready to serve through whatever task He puts in our path. The places or situations we are in may not be unexpected pregnancies but unexpected circumstances that bring about a long trial of unexplained circumstances. This unwanted and unexpected consequence can be a place of yielding, growing and serving or a place of lonely muteness. This is determined by our heart posture. Straighten your shoulders. Clean up your attitude. Tune your attention. Square up your heart posture to align with God's purpose.

Both pregnancies were unexpected in timing and the one prayed for was the one whose timing caused doubt. Do not allow God's timing to cause your heart to harbor doubt of who He is. This seed of unbelief is a dangerous place that needs to be cast out. Instead do as Jesus showed us through Mary and His own yielding, be it unto me as you have said. Heart posture equals trust in God's timing.

Get the word out. Teach all these things. And don't let anyone put you down because you're young. Teach believers with your life: by word, by demeanor, by love, by faith, by integrity. Stay at your post reading Scripture, giving counsel, teaching. And that special gift of ministry you were given when the leaders of the church laid hands on you and prayed—keep that dusted off and in use.

1 Timothy 4: 11-14

Post It!

Everyone is up right now as the weather was so rough that it woke us. Phones blowing up with alerts and lightning, wind and trees down all startle us awake. I jumped on social media and saw immediately that lots of people are up posting. They are getting the word out about their situation. God brought this scripture to heart at this moment. Our purpose and our ministry are unique to us. As I lay here typing this message, my husband is out ministering by clearing a tree from the road in our neighborhood. That is his specialty and his gift of ministry. None of us are the same with the same callings, gifts or abilities. Don't let anyone demean what you do because your purpose is unlike anyone else's purpose or calling. Elizabeth was purposed to be the mother of John the Baptist, and Mary, the mother of Jesus. Esther was purposed to be a queen and Ruth a widow gleaning in a field to meet her future. We don't always understand God's plans or purpose but it is our job to teach others by our lives. We are called and tasked to use our words, our demeanor, our love, our faith, our integrity and our abilities uniquely to lead others to know God. We are to stay at our post, our lane, our purpose doing what God has given to us to do. Each of us has special gifts of ministry that no one else has. Embrace the person God has tasked you to be just by doing what He puts before you. Maybe your job is to call and check on others, pray, encourage or exhort them. Maybe your job is to move a tree or maybe your purpose is to pray, teach, or just get the word out. God has uniquely gifted each of us unlike anyone else. Keep your ministries and gifts dusted off and in use for His purpose. Do not let the struggles of day to day keep you sidelined when He has purpose for you. I do not like bad weather so it stresses me out. During the midst of these storms, I had a couple of sweet people text to check on me. This is a ministry. Don't put down that moment or purpose. Those texts were like a hug from God saying I know you, see you and love you. This ministry was just a moment of time. These people may not even realize that God used them but it was a gift. Get the word out. God has purpose in you and in your gifting. Do not let anyone or anything deter you. He has purposed you! Get up! Dust off your gifts! Quit doubting His purpose in you. You are valued and uniquely purposed. I cannot minister by removing trees from roads and serving in that way but I can pray, post and encourage. Get busy! God has purposely called you!

"I tell you, love your enemies. Help and give without expecting a return. You'll never–I promise–regret it. Live out this God-created identity the way our Father lives toward us, generously and graciously, even when we're at our worst. Our Father is kind; you be kind.

Luke 6: 35-36

No Regrets!

Looking back at our lives, there are always things that we wish we would've done differently. From being more attentive to our kids, to spending more quality time, to not snapping, to finding more joy and on and on. The life of no regrets only comes in commitment to the Lord. Living His will is a life of no regrets in Him. We will always question whether we are good enough, strong enough, or flat just enough in everything as we are human but we do not have to question our choice in choosing Jesus. Being generous and gracious in our day to day is a trait of character of Jesus and through this there are no regrets. There is so much tension in people pulling and tugging every which way in life right now. If we will set our minds on Him and walk in His love, openly giving generously of ourselves without expecting people to pay us back in the way God created our identity to live, then we live the life of no regret. Our Father is kind, generous and gracious towards us even when we act poorly, at our worst. He expects us to show His character to those around us, especially to those we love and to His people. Generously living and loving is a characteristic of who He is. To live for God is to be His hand extended. To be blessed and live a life of no regrets takes putting your hand in His and not looking back. Regret and looking back only causes conflict and confusion. We cannot undo what we have done in the past but we can move forward in faith that He who does Good things is faithful to keep us despite our missteps and misdoing and misfortunes. No matter what, love. Love those who do you wrong and love those who love you well. A life of God's love is a life of no regrets.

"Count on it: The day is coming, raging like a forest fire. All the arrogant people who do evil things will be burned up like stove wood, burned to a crisp, nothing left but scorched earth and ash—a black day. But for you, sunrise! The sun of righteousness will dawn on those who honor my name, healing radiating from its wings. You will be bursting with energy, like colts frisky and frolicking. And you'll tromp on the wicked. They'll be nothing but ashes under your feet on that Day." God-of-the-Angel-Armies says so.

"Remember and keep the revelation I gave through my servant Moses, the revelation I commanded at Horeb for all Israel, all the rules and procedures for right living.

"But also look ahead: I'm sending Elijah the prophet to clear the way for the Big Day of God—the decisive Judgment Day! He will convince parents to look after their children and children to look up to their parents. If they refuse, I'll come and put the land under a curse."

Malachi 4: 1-6

Power Up!

As I sit here in the dark with cool air blowing over me, I hear the whine of the generators all over my neighborhood. The storm came and left destruction all over and the electric grid is suffering. My husband is having to work very hard to maintain the generator power watching the oil and gas, the amount of amperage being used and constant maintenance to keep the power rolling. It is a lot of work and vigilance. The crews are meanwhile working behind the scenes diligently trying to get the electrical grid back up from power lines to substations. In spiritual life situations, just like the physical, the storms keep rolling in and each frustrating thing mounts, wearing on the soul. We have to work to maintain our power making sure we are monitoring our amperage of output and staying full of anointing oil. We have to allow time for The Holy Spirit/God to work on the power grid in times of sudden and unexpected storms that take our feet from under us. His powers never stop but sometimes the lines between us may seem to have been disrupted by life. Sometimes it seems that He has quit working on our behalf but this is not the case. I especially love the story when the archangel Gabriel is headed to work on behalf of Daniel in Daniel chapter 10. He said no sooner had you prayed than I was headed your way but I was waylaid by the prince of persia and had to call Michael to come fight on my behalf so I could come to you. God of the Angel Armies is fighting for us. He says the sun of righteousness will dawn on those who honor His name, healing radiance coming on the wings and we will burst with energy tromping the wickedness to ashes under our feet. When the trials mount like storms and the days seem endless with frustration, we must remember who we are and that Christ Himself is working behind the scenes sending armies of angels to work and fight on our behalf. We must not give up but Count on it..that the day is coming like a firestorm. It may seem like only a small ember is left burning in you and that the flames of spirit are waning but they are hot coals. They will rekindle when the breath of God blows across them into a mighty firestorm. The power of His anointing is there. It hasn't left you deserted and alone. You are His. Remembering who you are and who He is keeps the coals hot until the time He blows them into flame. Maintain. Do not give up! He has big plans for you. The wind is picking up outside, I hear the warning sounds of a storm coming. But I also know that my husband is diligently working on the generator to correct the issues it is having with staying connected to the power source. He is laboring on my behalf today as God labors on behalf of all of us. The storms of life are raging but we must be about the Father's business constantly maintaining the power flow as He works to restore what the enemy has tried to take from us. Stay connected and in tune. Read His word, pray His promises and praise His greatness as He works on our behalf. He is coming soon in power and glory. The generator has kicked back on as I hear the humming and the melody that the refrigerator plays when it comes back to power. Tune your spiritual generator to His word and begin to hum and sing a melody of praise. He delights in our worship. Know that He is God and He is at work on our behalf.

Because of this decision we don't evaluate people by what they have or how they look. We looked at the Messiah that way once and got it all wrong, as you know. We certainly don't look at him that way anymore. Now we look inside, and what we see is that anyone united with the Messiah gets a fresh start, is created new. The old life is gone; a new life emerges! Look at it! All this comes from the God who settled the relationship between us and him, and then called us to settle our relationships with each other. God put the world square with himself through the Messiah, giving the world a fresh start by offering forgiveness of sins. God has given us the task of telling everyone what he is doing. We're Christ's representatives. God uses us to persuade men and women to drop their differences and enter into God's work of making things right between them. We're speaking for Christ himself now: Become friends with God; he's already a friend with you.

2 Corinthians 5: 16-20

Look Inside!

The tree was hollow and the roots looked a little like a monster. Nothing was there to sustain life so the wind blew and the tree toppled. What had been was no longer. I am sure many creatures had once lived in and on this tree. It had been a life source and a home but change had a way of taking from the tree and now it laid on the ground being cut up to be burned. In 2nd Corinthians, Paul writes to that body of believers about the importance of examining the inside not the outside of what people have or how they look. People looked upon Jesus and judged him wrongly because He hadn't come in riches and glory but humbly in a stable to a virgin of little means. Now we know that since Jesus makes all things new, we are not to judge on past experiences nor expectations but look inside for the fresh start. A fresh start, a clean slate, a new beginning are all possibilities through Christ Jesus. He is calling us to go into our marketplace of ministry and tell others of His love, sacrifice and atonement. He challenges us to make the way plain to settle our relationships with others as He put the world square with God through His sacrifice. He wants us to drop our differences and embrace the wholeness of who He is as we make things right between each of us. Paul says we speak for Christ Himself now persuading others to become friends with God for He is already friends with them. What is a friend? God says a True friend is one who is willing to lay down his life for another. In all of this storm season and lack of resources, especially electricity, it has been evident who is all about themselves and who is willing to be more. Giving up oneself for others is hard. It requires sacrifices of desire and pleasure, comfort and ease. As people fight to survive in situations like these, we see the challenges of staying in Him. Outside we may look like a good person but the inside is hollow and rotting waiting for a strong wind to topple us. If we hang around too long with the empty and hollow, then their demise is often ours, also, as happened with the trees. You see that hollow tree took out two trees with life in them as it fell because they were in its path and had intertwined roots with the dead tree. When the wind of God takes out the deadness, and hollow empty lives in our world, if we are intertwined with them, we may suffer the consequences of their fall. God instructs us to tell them of His love, live and walk loudly in His love but He does not want us to become a part of their wicked ways that have led to deadness. We are to be used of God to persuade people to drop their differences and enter into God's work of making things right. We are to settle our relationships and emerge through Him into new life not harboring any of the old. A butterfly lifts off flittering around me, reminding me that this new life came through willingness to sacrifice the old. The caterpillar had to create the cocoon and settle itself into that tomb in order to emerge as a new creature. Sometimes the situations of life feel like a tomb to us but if we are settled in Christ, we will emerge victorious with wings like eagles, we will run and not be weary and walk without fainting. We will be His people and His friends. Look inside. Are you living and growing in Him, settled to become what He wants you to be or are you rotting and dying inside because you have chosen yourself over His will? Examine it. Embrace the change. God is waiting on you to be His friend. He has offered His friendship to you through His sacrifice. He was willing to lay down His life for you. Are you willing to do the same for Him? Look inside.

Mary kept all these things to herself, holding them dear, deep within herself. The shepherds returned and let loose, glorifying and praising God for everything they had heard and seen. It turned out exactly the way they'd been told!

Luke 2: 19-20

Held Deep!

As I daily pack my things to prepare to move from this home to another, I touch and cradle things I haven't held in a while but have deep sentimental value. Letting go of things is hard for me but not so for my husband. He would be Marie Kondo's dream client. Letting go of things is easy for him as he enjoys decluttering. I, on the other hand, am very sentimental and place precious value on the things I have been blessed with as I can tell you the person and occasion upon which I received most of my things. Each precious memory is locked into a special place in my mind/heart so when I see a cherished item, it invokes deep thoughts of that moment and that person. Mary pondered on these things. I imagine she had a lot of things that she kept to herself and thought on, holding those thoughts and feelings close to her as dear, deep within her. Don't you know that she had periods of doubt and unease, fear and frustration during this time of carrying this Baby? I mean, here she is having God himself but cannot get a sanitary place to give birth, not even a place of shelter. I imagine that she really felt left alone with this huge, enormous burden. Joseph knew about it but there were obviously questions he had that he probably felt uncomfortable asking her and there were so many details left out as Mary pondered and didn't tell a lot. My mom reminds me of Mary because she is a quiet worker. She has the same spirit of whatever God puts before me, I will do without any questions. She has done things for others that I just shake my head at because I do not understand but she just quietly goes about the doing keeping her thoughts to herself most of the time. That's why she is so loved. Everyone knows my mom loves them and will do anything for them that they ask but rarely do people return that favor. Most people are all about themselves, especially Christians, even though they should be different. Most people I meet do not understand the quiet, holding things of God to themselves and working them out deep within themselves. Most people are just like the shepherds...let's throw a party because what God said would happen did happen. Mary was unique but I think that's why she was chosen to bear God's most precious gift to humanity. She had a gift that was a quiet spirit. She kept all these things to herself, holding them dear, deep within herself as she pondered on God. I am not against testimony nor am I against shouting about God's goodness. I wonder though, what would happen if we took more time to ponder what He is doing than to live in the highs and lows? Downsizing is not fun. Saying goodbye to treasures and things that hold memories and places that are dear is challenging to say the least. In this time of transition in my life, I am going to become more thoughtful about God's preponderance and less about my own. I am going to take time to think on these things in my heart and see if I can learn that holding dear and deep is more valuable than being the star of the show.

In Jerusalem at the time, there was a man, Simeon by name, a good man, a man who lived in the prayerful expectancy of help for Israel. And the Holy Spirit was on him. The Holy Spirit had shown him that he would see the Messiah of God before he died. Led by the Spirit, he entered the Temple. As the parents of the child Jesus brought him in to carry out the rituals of the Law, Simeon took him into his arms and blessed God: God, you can now release your servant; release me in peace as you promised. With my own eyes I've seen your salvation; it's now out in the open for everyone to see: A God-revealing light to the non-Jewish nations, and of glory for your people Israel. Jesus' father and mother were speechless with surprise at these words. Simeon went on to bless them, and said to Mary his mother,

Luke 2: 25-35

Failure and Recovery!

His frustration was palpable as he sat trying to conquer his emotions. The look of defeat on his face was heart wrenching. I sat beside him and asked what was wrong. He told me he just wanted a super power like telekinetic ability because his brothers were always winning the video games and making fun of him. While this may seem minor to us, to him, it was very important as it was defining him to himself. He wants to be a winner and doesn't like failure. We have all been in that place of failure and it isn't a fun place but it is a place of growing. Sometimes the place of waiting is perceived as failure. Simeon and Anna had both waited a long time in their lives. Simeon was an elderly Priest and Anna a prophetess and lowly widow of 84 years. She had been married for seven years then spent the last 84 years in the house of God praying. Simeon has been promised to see the Messiah before his death. Both were not at the pinnacles of society or life. Both were in a place of waiting and yet God had purposed that for them and us. Simeon's realization of who Jesus was immediately when he took him in his arms made Mary and Joseph speechless with surprise because Simeon revealed Jesus' purpose as a God-revealing light to the non-Jewish nations as well as the glory of the Jewish people. He continued by remarking that Jesus would be a misunderstood and contradicted figure-like a sword thrust through you as His rejection by the status quo would force honesty by God revealing who the "religious" really were. Political forces had taken hold of the church in that day and religious rites had become a political football. It was this political machine that crucified Jesus but only because He chose to follow the way of the cross to bring about the failure and recovery of it all, to be the once and for all sacrifice. Anna saw this all and celebrated by telling all in the temple area that the Messiah had come. Failure and recovery. Neither of these are fun aspects of life as they both require loss and waiting, patience and fortitude. As I sat with that little guy at my office and explained that telekinetic ability wouldn't change his thinking, only failure and recovery would, I felt God wing that exact message into my heart. It is through the breaking that we learn. It is through the falling, the failure, the loss, the hurt, the pain, the storms and the waiting places that we learn to grow in him and root deeper in Him. The sorrows of this life only bring about a breaking because they lead to a recovery. We can choose to feel defeated at the loss and failure or we can choose to begin rejoicing in that moment or waiting place as we know victory is coming. Things may not always play out like we think they will. Loss, sorrow, pain and failure will come to us all but through these places, we learn to get back up and try again. I told him he had a superpower but it wasn't telekinetic ability. It was grit. Grit comes from the failures and the learnings. It is a skill that predicts success because you learn from the deep, dark, waiting places. He began to smile. I told him to embrace failure as a learning place and watch his skills begin to grow and become. I cannot wait to see the change in him as he goes through brain training because I know the confidence and learning of what's on the other side as I have seen it with so many. God is doing the same for us. He put a cheer-leader named Anna in the church for 84 years praying and waiting on Jesus to come. She thought her purpose was over when she became a widow but she had just walked into her purpose. Simeon was tired and felt like giving up on ministry but God had a purpose and timing for him too. You may be exhausted in the struggle and feel defeated in circumstances but know that God has you in this time for a purpose. This place of waiting and growing is as import-ant to you as it is for the seed in that dark deep ground. It is in this waiting that He is using the failures of life to bring about recovery. Embrace it as a growing place. Praise and pray, sing and rejoice for He is working this in us.

The next day they found him in the Temple seated among the teachers, listening to them and asking questions. The teachers were all quite taken with him, impressed with the sharpness of his answers. But his parents were not impressed; they were upset and hurt. His mother said, "Young man, why have you done this to us? Your father and I have been half out of our minds looking for you."
He said, "Why were you looking for me? Didn't you know that I had to be here, dealing with the things of my Father?" But they had no idea what he was talking about.
So he went back to Nazareth with them, and lived obediently with them. His mother held these things dearly, deep within herself. And Jesus matured, growing up in both body and spirit, blessed by both God and people.

Luke 2: 46-52

Body and Spirit!

Submission and obedience are very important to God. It is evident in this scripture. Jesus is a young man who knows who He is and His authority. He acts in His authority and decides to stay behind in the temple teaching when His earthly parents head home. Of course, when they discover this, after the panic and frustration of looking for Him, they are irritated and hurt by His behavior. While all the teachers in the Temple are impressed with Him, His parents see Him as their son who was not in line with what they desired Him to do. His mother scolds Him and He responds but they were in an earthly mindset of parenting so didn't comprehend what Jesus was saying. Here He chooses submissive obedience. In Luke, it says they had no idea what He was talking about so He went back to Nazareth with them and lived obediently. His mother held these things dearly and deeply as Jesus matured, growing in body and spirit, blessed by God and people. I know I desire to be blessed by God and people as well as mature in body and spirit. Submissive obedience is the key. Often we may feel like we know best or truly have the right answers but the key to blessings is submissive obedience. Often in life when I know more than others about a particular subject or field, I desire to show or demonstrate what I know and this can get me into trouble. I remember a story about a rancher and a game warden. The game warden came onto the rancher's property and asserted his authority. He said he was going to search a field for bait. The rancher said "You don't want to do that", but the game warden showed his badge and said "This says I can". The rancher quietly allowed the game warden to do as he desired and shortly a rampaging bull was chasing the game warden. As he hollered and ran, the rancher said, "Show him your badge". Obviously the bull did not care. The point of the story is that often we barge into situations we have no knowledge of and can end up causing ourselves grief and pain that could have been prevented if we had been submissive and listened obediently. Jesus had and has all authority. He could easily have over ridden his earthly parents' rules and desires but He demonstrated for us submission. He put His authority on hold to learn the ways of man so He could in all points understand our temperament and temptations. He learned and lived obediently from His earthly parents although I am sure He knew much more than they did about things. The purpose of submissive obedience is that it teaches us the process of learning and leaning. The best students, employees and best leaders are those who have learned submissive obedience. It is often a hard lesson that causes failures and frustrations. Recently I had a young man argue and argue to have his way about things during his brain training session. I allowed him his moment to "do it his way" then we did it again the correct way. He then asked me why I had not argued with him and allowed him to do it his way as it was a waste of time. I told him I wasn't the one who wasted his time. He wanted to do it his way so I allowed it but then we did it the correct way. Often, God allows us this same manner. I look at stories in the Bible such as Abraham who had enormous faith but yet doubted God could give him a son as promised so he decided to help God and created a problem we are all still dealing with today. God allowed it and then still provided His promise in His time. How often we waste time by "having it our way" instead of submissively obeying and waiting on Him. Maybe today we should hold this lesson dear and deep within us: Jesus, God's own son submitted to his parents' authority in obedience to teach us that submissive obedience is the key to blessings. What are we "doing our own way" today instead of being submissively obedient to Him about?

When crowds of people came out for baptism because it was the popular thing to do, John exploded: "Brood of snakes! What do you think you're doing slithering down here to the river? Do you think a little water on your snakeskins is going to deflect God's judgment? It's your life that must change, not your skin. And don't think you can pull rank by claiming Abraham as 'father.' Being a child of Abraham is neither here nor there—children of Abraham are a dime a dozen. God can make children from stones if he wants. What counts is your life. Is it green and flourishing? Because if it's deadwood, it goes on the fire."

Luke 3: 7-9

Skin Shedding!

I watched the car going back-and-forth, back-and-forth, back-and-forth in front of my driveway. I wondered what was going on and then I realized that my neighbor next-door was trying to kill a snake with her car. The next morning I walked out expecting to see a dead snake in the road in front of my driveway. Instead, I saw only a snake skin. In this chapter of Luke, as I was reading, John called the people who came to baptize only because it was the popular thing to do, a brood of snakes. He says that throwing a little water on their snakeskins was not going to deflect God's judgment on them. They were not willing to change their lifestyles, nor change their ways but they wanted to fit in and make sure they covered all the bases. We see this a lot in our culture today where people are enthralled with getting baptized and posting it on Facebook and doing it over and over to cover their bases, but they have no intent in changing their life at all. They go through the motions only because it is a popular thing to do. Yesterday I spoke to a mother, who was so excited that her son had decided to get re-baptized. I asked the child what had made him decide that this was the time that he decided to change. He said, oh no I'm not making any changes, everyone else was doing it, so I thought I might as well. This is exactly what is happening with many people, trying to cover their bases, yet still not making any change. They want to live the life that they have been living, but they want to make sure, just in case, that they've dipped their toes in the water of God's love. When I arrived home yesterday, there was smoke everywhere, because my husband was burning green tree debris. Green trees do not burn easily. In fact, they are almost impossible to burn as the water that is in them will put out the fire. The only quick way to burn them is to put them with a lot of deadwood. Deadwood burns hotter and will eventually dry out the green wood that is cut from the tree and burn it up. As he burned, I was concerned about the trees that were around the burn pile. I asked him if it was safe to burn right there. He told me absolutely because those trees had enough living water in them that they would not catch fire because his fire was not hot enough as it was full of green wood, which was what produced all the smoke. What do our lives produce? Are we fruitful and productive or are we deadwood? Are we easily burned up or green and flourishing? John stated that God can make children of stones if He wants. God can make rocks and trees cry out His praise. He wants us to do so with a willing heart and not a "because it is the thing to do" mindset. What is your motivation to serve? Are you serving from habit and just skin shedding or are you becoming a new creature in Him? Which are you, snake or caterpillar?

Now Jesus, full of the Holy Spirit, left the Jordan and was led by the Spirit into the wild. For forty wilderness days and nights he was tested by the Devil. He ate nothing during those days, and when the time was up he was hungry. Jesus answered by quoting Deuteronomy: "It takes more than bread to really live." Jesus refused, again backing his refusal with Deuteronomy: "Worship the Lord your God and only the Lord your God. Serve him with absolute single-heartedness." "Yes," said Jesus, "and it's also written, 'Don't you dare tempt the Lord your God.'" That completed the testing. The Devil retreated temporarily, lying in wait for another opportunity.

Luke 4: 1-2, 4, 8, 12-13

Tempting Opportunity!

I saw the glint in his eye and the grin upon his face as he prepared to jump into the pool splashing his grandmother thoroughly. She sensed it also and she said, you go right ahead and see what happens...he moved a little further away and jumped to lessen the splash but still make sure she got some. She has no extra eyes in the back of her head nor does she have extra sensory perception. She's been an educator for over 30 years and a grandmother over ten as well as being a mom of a man-child. I say this as I know the glint that the Devil must've had in his eye as he thought he had the upper hand. But Jesus wasn't just the Son of God and Son of Man at this moment. Jesus was full of the Holy Ghost and had just been with God flowing through Him declaring Him His son. Jesus walked into the wilderness temptation of 40 days full of anointing but He left it full of confidence because He allowed the Greater to become Greater. The first temptation test flows back to Jacob/Esau as Esau gave up his birthright blessing for food when he was hungry. Jesus clearly states that bread isn't the only way to live, making us know the spiritual trumps the physical and conquering the physical to obtain the spiritual is an important place of growth. So often we fail to recognize this in our own lives. We allow our physical limitations or situations to keep us from receiving the blessings of God because we limit His hand in our lives by accepting the temporal rather than waiting on the miracle. The miracle is often already in the making but we rush in messing up what God is doing. The second temptation test was to worship the creation instead of the Creator. Often we get caught up sacrificing time and money to attend concerts and events worshiping people who are stars but then we are too tired to worship God. We spend hours in lines to await entertainment of all types but cannot wait patiently ten minutes at church. We endure all kinds of inconveniences for our own pleasure but we will not wait patiently on God. Instead Jesus instructs using the Word, Serve the Lord Our God with absolute single mindedness! Not a divided heart and mind but fully embracing who He is in all aspects of our lives. Then the third testing was given to throw Himself into a bad situation and call angels to rescue Him. In all of these, Jesus could have done the God thing and conquered them but He was demonstrating to us that we must live above the fray. As He says, it is written, we are reminded that the Truth is powerfully written for us. Better than any magical spell or fairy godmother created by man's imagination, God's word imbues power from God Himself. Often we put ourselves in danger and in situations because we missed the first two lessons and allowed fleshly desires and indulgences to take us to where God never desired us to be, then we holler out for God to save us. I remember John as a young toddler crying Momma save me and I could hear him but couldn't find him. He had used the refrigerator as a ladder and climbed onto the tall cabinets above the fridge to look down but now he could not find a way down. As he looked below, he knew he needed help. I think God and the butt warming I gave him after getting him down inspired the fear of heights he now has to this day! Satan comes at us as he came to Jesus with loads of temptations and while we concentrate on these three tests because they tested core principles of doctrine, the scriptures clearly state that Jesus was tempted and tried and tested for 40 days before these recorded tests and it finishes with "the Devil retreated temporarily, lying in wait for another opportunity." Temptations and testings are a part of life. They come at unexpected times and certainly come with the intention of deterring us from His purposes. We must keep our eyes on these truths: We are eternal beings so do not let fleshly desires steal your future. We are first and foremost purposed with worshiping God above all else, so that means choosing church over baseball or cheer or others. And we are not to tempt God by putting ourselves into situations He would not have us be in. Finally we must know that the Devil is a roaring lion and it may seem that he is in control, he sure thinks so, but Greater is He that is in Me than the little ole Devil. Temptation is a test but there will never come a test in our lives that we do not have the way out or cheat sheet of answers to because we know the Master Creator of the Winds and Waves. Yes, it may seem like the trial is overwhelming and going on forever but get your eyes off the temporal and onto Him, the author and finisher of our faith.

He answered, "I suppose you're going to quote the proverb, 'Doctor, go heal yourself. Do here in your hometown what we heard you did in Capernaum.' Well, let me tell you something: No prophet is ever welcomed in his hometown. Isn't it a fact that there were many widows in Israel at the time of Elijah during that three and a half years of drought when famine devastated the land, but the only widow to whom Elijah was sent was in Sarepta in Sidon? And there were many lepers in Israel at the time of the prophet Elisha but the only one cleansed was Naaman the Syrian."

That set everyone in the meeting place seething with anger. They threw him out, banishing him from the village, then took him to a mountain cliff at the edge of the village to throw him to his doom, but he gave them the slip and was on his way.

Luke 4: 23-30

Hometown Doom!

How do people go from being enthralled with God to disgusted with him so quickly? Why is there so little trust, so much lack of faith, and so much frustration with God, when we rarely do our part? As I was studying my lesson to teach in Children's church this morning, I was reading about Macedonia and learning so many new things. I began to think about Paul, and other people who God blessed and used, and then I read this passage in Luke. Here Jesus had just spoken at the church that morning, and everybody was excited about what He had to share, thrilled with Him, and then they began to ask questions which He answered. But they didn't like His answers, and quickly, they turned on Him, ready to throw Him over a cliff. Just because they didn't like the truth. How often are we just like this? God comes to us with hard truths and realities, but we don't like them so we are ready to toss out all we know because He didn't do what we wanted Him to do in the timeframe we wanted him to do it. If you look at this passage, you will see that Jesus says no prophet is ever welcomed in his hometown. He gives examples of Elijah and Elisha. He knew the people only saw him as the person he was as a child, and could not accept him as God Himself. How often do we relegate God to a box in our life-to the person we perceive him to be? Why do we limit him to what we think he can do or only what we want him to do? Who is God? Is He only what you think and what you want or what I think and I want? Let's face it, someone is always going to be disappointed. One person can be praying for the rain to come in the same town another person is praying for the rain not to come. One person is praying for something to happen, that's good in their favor, while in another person's favor they're praying against it. Only God knows what is best because he can get above the fray to look down and see the full picture of what He intends. When we get bogged down, we see only our own circumstances, and we fail to see what others need. Remember, He's God of all. If you cannot accept His will and His truths for what they are, then you, like these people in the passage, will want to throw Him out of your life because of the realities of your situation. Embracing God, means embracing whatever His will is, even if it is not what you would like. Yes, we definitely should pray. Yes, we definitely should intercede for other people and ourselves. But we must also realize that God has supreme authority, and His truth remains no matter what our opinion is. Why God chose one thing one way or another may not be answered this side of Heaven. We may not know why a loved one died or a situation was allowed to happen. We may know and not like the reason or circumstances but our situational feelings do not change Who He is. In His hometown, He went from celebrity to doomed in minutes. How fickle we are as a people if we celebrate God only when things go our way. Opening our eyes to His ways is allowing Him to be God in the good and the bad, in the hard truths and the joys, in the lowest of lows and highest of highs. God is God no matter whether we accept it or not but by embracing Who He is, we get a glimpse of His glory and learn that He is for us. As I prepare to attend the LearningRx yearly convention, I think of the celebrations nationally for the hard work we have put in. I know we will be celebrated there, although we are rarely acknowledged here in our hometown after 15 years of service. Why? Because people just see you as you. They don't see the full picture. They don't see outside the scope. You can be a celebrity to the world and ignored in your hometown, but to God, you are His. You can be a failure to the world or not even acknowledged but to God, you are His. This is the Hometown Doom and Gloom or Hometown Bloom. You choose. God doesn't rely on our opinion of His abilities to function but He does work miracles on our behalf when we choose to embrace who He is through the good and the bad. Don't let your status in life define who you are. God is God and He is for You! Don't let your feelings or failures define you. God is God and He is For You! If God's own son was ignored with His miraculous ways, you can be certain that people will let you down. Quit allowing it! God is God. He didn't fail and He won't stop. Their anger did nothing to Him but they missed out on the blessings because of it. Let it Go! Trust Him!

Distress that drives us to God does that. It turns us around. It gets us back in the way of salvation. We never regret that kind of pain. But those who let distress drive them away from God are full of regrets, end up on a deathbed of regrets.

2 Corinthians 7:10

Distressed Turn!

Driving down the road one day, my mind was on other things, until suddenly a dog ran in front of the car toward the field of horses. I had to swerve, but wait, now his owner is in the road too, and as I braked, I had to choose not to hit the man or the dog. In much distress, I turned my car around because my choice had not been without consequences. My heart was broken and hurting as the man looked at me in tears carrying his dog back to his yard. My heart was completely broken too. No one wants to make hard choices like this. No one wants to see an animal hurt, injured or maimed. I knew the vet across the street and the dog could go there but alas, it was too late. As the family mourned their loss, they told me of the moment of decision to let the dog off the leash on that busy road to run free with the horses. Their hearts and voices were full of regret as they related the decision to me. I too had regrets. I had unintentionally harmed an animal of God's creation but my choice given was an impossible one with no other options. I could not leave the road and I had to choose the path of man or dog as one was in one lane and the other followed in the other lane. Split second decisions at high rates of speed. I am so grateful that another car was not passing at that same moment on that busy road lest all of us be gone. That one moment has changed the way I approach that particular stretch of road. Now I pray for these people and I see they have a new dog that remains on the leash as she chases the horses now. Distress comes in many forms in our lives. Hard circumstances and impossible situations can drive us to our knees or away from God. It is our choice. If we allow distressed times to motivate us to turn around and get back on the path of salvation or to tune back in from the distractions of life, then we never regret that kind of pain. In 2018, I went through horrible sickness and pain but I have no regrets because that pain made my marriage and my business stronger. It weathered us in ways I cannot explain as it drove us deeper in relationships and reliance on one another. If distress and hardships come to tune your life into His ways, do not allow the distractions and disturbances to pull you out to the deep away from His love. Lean into Him and allow Him to buffer you from the storms so that your edges are smoothed and rounded but you are not broken with regret. A stone in a river of God's love will still experience tossing, turning, tumbling and rolling as the water carries it but it will become as God intended, a smooth, rounded piece of His glory that settles into a place of joy when the stone has run its course. We may feel like we are being persecuted, tumbled, taken down and destroyed but we must remember that He is the Master and if we trust Him, our distress will turn us back into the way of salvation, which leads us to being settled in His love as those rough edges are knocked away in the waterfalls of life and God's love. We have purposes which God has determined. We must yield and allow ourselves to be guided by Him through the stress into the calm waters of rest. He keeps us safe from the storms even as they seem to overtake us. There is purpose in the storm. Allow the distress to drive you to God not away. Choose wisely.

God holds me head and shoulders
above all who try to pull me down.
I'm headed for his place to offer anthems
that will raise the roof!
Already I'm singing God-songs;
I'm making music to God.
Listen, God, I'm calling at the top of my lungs:
"Be good to me! Answer me!"
When my heart whispered, "Seek God,"
my whole being replied,
"I'm seeking him!"
Don't hide from me now!
You've always been right there for me;
don't turn your back on me now.
Don't throw me out, don't abandon me;
you've always kept the door open.
My father and mother walked out and left me,
but God took me in.
I'm sure now I'll see God's goodness
in the exuberant earth.
Stay with God!
Take heart. Don't quit.
I'll say it again:
Stay with God.

Psalms 27:6-9, 13-14

Exuberant Earth!

Head and shoulders above all who try to pull me down! This is where God holds me. He holds me in a place to offer anthems and praises, a place to make music and sing at the top of my lungs of His goodness through the trials. God's goodness is evident in the song of the birds, the trill of the cicadas and the beauty of the sunset. Seeing God's goodness is a choice. We can look at the ground and miss the rainbow. We can feel the heat and miss the breeze of His breath. We can hear the noise and miss the melody in the creatures singing His praises. We can smell the stench of Earth and miss the fragrance of the flowers. It is all a choice. God holds us head and shoulders above all, not for our glory but for His praises. If we choose to not praise, He can raise the rocks to the pinnacles of praise. Making music to God and seeing His hand in all that is in our lives is a choice. In the good times, that choice is easier than in the bad times but jewels are not grown in the open. They grow under pressure in the dark. Coal becomes diamonds or oil, both of extreme value as is the coal. We concentrate on value rather than the process. We get caught up in the outcome rather than the making but it is in the making that the beauty is truly seen. I always like watching a groom see His bride for the first time because it is a culmination of all the preparation, but that is the beginning of the marriage. The truth is that the process matters and we often fail to see the process as having value. A storm can be scary and overwhelming but the pieces of the storms of life didn't happen all at once. There was a process and understanding the process often helps us to understand the storm and to weather it better. There are often unexpected things in storms from hail to high winds to tornadoes but the storm itself came with expected rain, thunder and lightning. These factors are often overlooked as they are always there in the storms but these are the making of the storm. I remember counting between lightning to thunder to tell how far away a storm is, in fact I still do this sometimes. The fact is that in knowledge there is confidence. If we know who God is in the storm and we see His hand at work through the storm, then we have confidence even through the unexpected uncertainty that comes. The Earth recognizes God as the Creator whether man does or doesn't. The music of worship through the storms of life comes from the confidence of knowing this. I am amazed to hear the trill of nature through the storms that have been through here recently. Much wildlife was displaced and upended by the fall of trees and change of course in the storms and yet, the song of the birds continues just as it was the day before. Why? Because they are confident in the Creator. David wrote this song in confidence of who God is. He tells his heart to be encouraged because He knows He will see God's goodness on the exuberance of Earth and it will remind him to take heart, don't quit and stay with God. If you feel down and feel like God has forgotten you, step into nature, listen, smell, feel, hear and see His exuberance in the Earth and know He is God. Join your voice with the song of the bird and the trill of the cicada. Know that He is holding you head and shoulders above all that tries to pull you down! Offer an anthem of praise in confidence of who He is!

Jesus knew exactly what they were thinking and said, "Why all this gossipy whispering? Which is simpler: to say 'I forgive your sins,' or to say 'Get up and start walking'? Well, just so it's clear that I'm the Son of Man and authorized to do either, or both. . . ." He now spoke directly to the paraplegic: "Get up. Take your bedroll and go home." Without a moment's hesitation, he did it—got up, took his blanket, and left for home, giving glory to God all the way. The people rubbed their eyes, stunned—and then also gave glory to God. Awestruck, they said, "We've never seen anything like that!"

Luke 5: 22-26

Authority Simplified!

As a business owner, the most simplistic method of getting something signed in my absence is a signature stamp. This carries my authority as it is my signature but it can be used by others so must only be trusted to those who are worthy to know my will. Jesus as God's son knew the thoughts of those questioning Him in this passage in Luke and knew that they didn't think He had authority so He demonstrated that He had authority through healing the paraplegic man fully then asked which was simpler, the forgiveness of sin or the healing. The issue isn't that both were equally easy for Christ. The issue is that the people had such a concept of sin that they believed the only authority to forgive came through sacrifice and they did not recognize Jesus' authority in this realm. We have a simplified view also. In fact, we might have the opposite viewpoint in that we recognize His power to forgive sin and accept it more easily than we recognize His ability to overcome the world as far as sickness, disease, etc. We often fail to recognize His authority for what it is, as we walk in the "reality" of life. The men who brought this sick friend to Jesus recognized His authority to heal. They raised the roof literally in order to put their friend before Jesus. They let nothing stand in their way in approaching Him. They saw the crowd and knew it was impossible to get through so they found a way to get His attention. God's authority is not limited by us but His attention to our needs can be enhanced through our approach. The ability to heal this man was always there in Jesus as well as the ability to forgive but the approach mattered. Reaching out through obstacles and seemingly impossible situations to Jesus who holds all authority in Heaven And Earth is how this man received his healing and his forgiveness but he could not do it by himself. He needed his friends to bring him before the king of all creation. He needed them to act on his behalf. This is where miracles occur. The faith not only of this man but of his friends in bringing him before Jesus and pushing through despite their own personal obstacles on behalf of their friend shows us an example of intercession. Intercession is the willingness to put aside personal convenience to approach the throne of grace on behalf of another. There is nothing else so powerful as the willingness of a friend to lay down their life for another. This is the example Christ gave. He laid down His life in simple and perfect sacrifice for atonement of our sins. He fulfilled the law through this. These friends laid down their conveniences and moved the roof to interrupt Jesus on behalf of their friend because they understood that He was authorized to heal even when they didn't recognize His authority to save from sin. Which is easier or more simple, Jesus asked: To say I forgive your sins or you are healed? As I lay here typing this message, my nerves are burning excruciatingly bad in my body, arms, legs and back. The pain is so bad that I just want to cry and yet I know that all authority has been given to me through Him whose sacrifice is supreme to approach the throne of grace. I can come before the throne in His simple authority knowing that as I raise the roof with praise, I am brought before the King of Glory who is able to forgive me and cleanse me as well as heal me. I understand His authority simplified! I know His ability to forgive is not outstripped by His ability to heal. I know I have friends and family who are lifting the roof with me, bringing me before Jesus and asking Him to heal me. This is intercession. Jesus knows exactly what we are thinking. He knows our doubts, fears and weaknesses but He is enough. Awestruck they were by the healing of this man and yet they failed to recognize the bigger miracle was the forgiveness of his sin. Keep approaching the throne over and over for your healing without doubting that He desires to heal you and recognizing that He has done much more through His forgiveness of our sins. His grace is enough. Lean in. These mortal homes we have are but temporary houses but the true authentic healing has already happened through salvation. Begin to walk in His authority and know that by His stripes we are healed as He works His salvation within us. God is in the healing business whether it be physical, mental, spiritual or emotional healings needed. And as I wrote, the pain resolved in my nerves and back because bringing it to Him matters.

At about that same time he climbed a mountain to pray. He was there all night in prayer before God. The next day he summoned his disciples; from them he selected twelve he designated as apostles:

Luke 6: 12-14

Prayer Pattern!

My mind is heavy with decisions both big and small. Sometimes my heart feels weighted, so I take it up to God in prayer. Many of us think that Jesus prayed and struggled with God's will only at the Garden of Gethsemane. The truth is that was the battle, but He has trained for that battle by taking it up in prayer many times before. In Luke chapter 6, we see one example where He climbed a mountain to pray all night before He made a momentous decision of calling His apostles. He had many disciples or followers but He prayed for wisdom before choosing these He was to bring closest to Him. I imagine He knew one of them would be a betrayer and a deceiver as He knew the things to come, so that struggling in prayer was intense. Often decisions we must make are weighty and hard. We struggle to balance the decisions and the problems. We worry and fret, sigh and puzzle when we clearly have an example of a better way. Choosing our advisors or people we trust to pull close and share our burdens requires wisdom and guidance. Knowing who we can go to in time of need is important and being wise about where we air our laundry is also. God is omnipotent and He knows us better than we know ourselves. He demonstrated by example while here on Earth that prayer is the place of decision making and that praying isn't a one and done nor a simple process when making big decisions. Decisions we make affect our lives a lot. Lately my husband and I have talked a lot about decisions we made and regret. Most of those were done in haste and without time spent together in prayer. Every decision we make has value and when it is time to make them, we should spend time praying before we jump. If God's son prayed all night long before choosing who would represent Him and who He would allow to draw close to Him as apostles receiving divine authority from Him to perform miracles and minister, then who are we to do less. We are called, we are given examples and we are taught to follow The Word. Several friends lately have been distracted and distressed over negative behaviors of men of God who made poor choices in life and fell into sin. Some of these men have done horrible things that disrespected and disregarded everything they had stood for in their lives, but the truth is that had they been taking their decisions of acquaintances to God in prayer, these things would not have happened. Temptation to sin comes from affiliation with sin. All of us will be tempted but scriptures tell us there is always a way of escape and scripture demonstrates that The Word is that way. In these days, it is best for all of us to stay prayed up and in The Word because there is a plethora of things that will distract us from Him. Big and small decisions require us to take it to God in prayer. He will meet us there and help us make our decisions in accordance with His will. Take it to Jesus!

Think of yourselves the way Christ Jesus thought of himself. He had equal status with God but didn't think so much of himself that he had to cling to the advantages of that status no matter what. Not at all. When the time came, he set aside the privileges of deity and took on the status of a slave, became human! Having become human, he stayed human. It was an incredibly humbling process. He didn't claim special privileges. Instead, he lived a selfless, obedient life and then died a selfless, obedient death—and the worst kind of death at that—a crucifixion.

Philippians 2: 5-8

Royal Advantage!

Taking advantage of privilege or using your network connections to advance in life is a normal approach to progress. In Philippians, Paul is writing to the church to think of themselves in a difficult way. He is telling them to follow the example of Christ and choose service over advancement via political gain. Here he shows us how Jesus who had equal status with God humbles Himself to become man which is one thing but then He chose to live an obedient, humble and I will say hard, sacrificial life all the way through to His death on the cross. Never once did He whine or say God has disappointed me or I have had enough of this. He lived humbly through the burdens and hardships, praying diligently for wisdom and guidance although He had it all at His command. I have to say that I would be terribly bad at being God because I am not as patient, loving and compassionate as He. When people do me wrong or hurt children or my family/friends, well.., it is a good thing I am not the powerful Almighty. I pray for them a lot. I do. I pray all kinds of things into their lives-let's just say I hope they like spiders and snakes! Then I have to repent and do as scripture instructs us through Christ. He endured even through death by crucifixion. He gladly took on that place for us because He knows us and yet He still loves us. Yesterday as we talked about power and privilege, one person relayed how unfair it is that some just seem to get everything handed to them while others have to strive so hard. This applies to all kinds of privileged things from IQ to EQ to SQ. Privilege reigns in our world. It isn't fair. It is a corrupt world. We are called to be different. We are called to be a light. We are called to humble ourselves and take on the lowly roles so that Christ can elevate us in His time and way. A diamond that is unpolished is still the same in value but the beauty has not yet been revealed. Our value isn't determined by our sparkle. The purpose of the sparkle is to draw lights and reflect it. We may feel like a dirty gem that has not gotten the uplift or privileges of others but we are no less in value. In His time, He will polish us to brilliantly shine His glory to all. Don't fret the times of humbleness. The polishing stone takes all the sparkle away during the process as it removes impurities and cleanses each little facet to glow internally. Selfless obedience is the way to achieve royal advancement. Doesn't mean you shouldn't network or connect with others, it means you should lift them up no matter what the cost to yourself. Humbleness is the path of greatness.

"Is there anyone here who, planning to build a new house, doesn't first sit down and figure the cost so you'll know if you can complete it? If you only get the foundation laid and then run out of money, you're going to look pretty foolish. Everyone passing by will poke fun at you: 'He started something he couldn't finish.'
"Or can you imagine a king going into battle against another king without first deciding whether it is possible with his ten thousand troops to face the twenty thousand troops of the other? And if he decides he can't, won't he send an emissary and work out a truce? "Simply put, if you're not willing to take what is dearest to you, whether plans or people, and kiss it good-bye, you can't be my disciple. "Salt is excellent. But if the salt goes flat, it's useless, good for nothing. "Are you listening to this? Really listening?"

Luke 14: 28-35

Decisions, Decisions!

As I spoke with my publisher and designer, I had many decisions to make. Writing is a passion of mine that I enjoy but making it look appealing to others and marketing it are not my strengths so sometimes these things overwhelm me and I just cannot decide. While writing the 15th book in the series is the plan today, I began to focus on the true purpose behind the writing once again. I write because God has given me a word to share. The combination or collection of these thoughts are gathered into a book and published so that others might enjoy them offline in other locations. Essentially, the purpose is sharing God's word with others. As Jesus spoke to the disciples in Luke, He illustrated to them the importance of planning to sacrifice. He knew the plan of God was for Him to give His life as an atonement and He was willing to choose this. Look at the things dearest to you. Are you willing to lay those things down for His glory? He asks His disciples if they were fully listening to what He was saying because He wanted them to grasp this importance. Planning and decisions for our future here is important and should be done but we must be willing to abandon all to follow Him if called to do so. Decisions about things must be made but sometimes things change, circumstances change, situations change and then we must adjust to the new reality to move forward. Our lives are not our own. We belong to God and He directs the wind in our sails of our lifeboat. He is the one who can open doors and windows as well as close them. Making plans to move forward in prayerful consideration is His way. I remember the day my son told me he had decided to join the National Guard. I knew in my heart that this was not the right path for him but it was not my decision to make so I prayed that God would move the goalposts if that was not His will. My son prepared and prepped as he always does to diligently be ready, then the big day arrived. I couldn't be there as I had to work so I prayed diligently. A few hours later he called and said that due to some unforeseen circumstances, he had changed his mind. This to me was a miracle that God had directly intervened in his life. He was unsure what was next but God has continued to guide him as He does each of us. One day we are wondering if He cares and the next, He dumps a blessing in our laps. Our plans when yielded to Him are always the best. As we pray for direction, it is like hiring a professional in the field. He has a perfect design. He has the provenance and provision to make it fully work out in His time. Our job is to trust and obey. Awake each morning and do as He instructs for that day. Do not borrow worry about tomorrow but trust that He has a plan for us as we walk throughout His purpose. I pray for each day that God speaks to me and to others through His word, allowing me to be a conduit of His love and truth. That is our purpose. One day and one decision at a time achieving His purpose in our lives. Plan ahead and be willing to adjust your sails to His plans for you.

Servants, do what you're told by your earthly masters. And don't just do the minimum that will get you by. Do your best. Work from the heart for your real Master, for God, confident that you'll get paid in full when you come into your inheritance. Keep in mind always that the ultimate Master you're serving is Christ. The sullen servant who does shoddy work will be held responsible. Being a follower of Jesus doesn't cover up bad work.

Colossians 3: 22-25

Mindset Matters!

Have you ever done a task you don't like when you are irritated? The task itself isn't the problem but easily becomes an issue because the emotion has taken reign. Overcoming mindset matters. If our mind is fixed on our situation, it is hard to see opportunities around us. When we become involved in a struggle, overwhelmed by our circumstances or emotionally overloaded then we cannot do the simplest things without losing our minds and hearts to the smallest inconvenience. Tiredness, defeat, frustration, irritation, disappointment, sadness and many other feelings can lead us to the place of negative mindset which drives us to make poor life decisions. Often, this can be in how we approach our jobs, causing conflict in our workplace. As a boss, a business owner and even a mom/wife, church leader, etc., I have found the role of service and servant leader to be the role that removes the hurt and frustration in lives. When I am caught up in my own issues and unable to assist or hear others, the workplace connections destabilize and become fraught with tension but when I remember my place to lead by example, the functional relationships of the workplace are beautiful and cohesive. Working from the heart for God in all we do means we do our very best in complete love and sacrifice with no other motive. It means we know that our purpose isn't about the dollar but about the Saving. It is evident in an employee and a boss when their mindset is selfish and all about them. They are intrinsically unmotivated and ungrateful while blaming others constantly for their own mistakes. Being coachable or willing to learn is the place of doing more than bare minimum. It is the place of growth and opportunity. It is the mindset of success and sustainability. Paul instructs the people in the letter of Colossians that mindset towards our work matters. Mindset is the key to conquering the hard places. It is the place of contentment instead of contention which leads to promotion through service. The all about me mindset defeats the reason and causes conflict. It can be hard to work for and with contentious people as they are never happy but scripture tells us that the heart of the servant who serves as if he/she is serving God Himself will be rewarded in due time. As an employer, I can truly say that promoting those who are willing to serve and give is much easier than those who are takers. In fact, those who are takers are job hoppers. They are never content and rarely stick with anything for any length of time. Having the mindset of Christ means being willing to walk through the tough places for eternal reward. I am so grateful to say that my staff are all servant leaders. This makes a huge difference to others in the willingness to see change and work to be the difference. Evaluate your roles in life. Where are you willing to serve instead of being served? Are you taking on the mindset of Christ or being selfish in your roles of employment? Are you busy at work for The Master or too busy complaining about your role in life? Mindset matters. Lead by example and watch the results.

I found myself in trouble and went looking for my Lord;
my life was an open wound that wouldn't heal.
When friends said, "Everything will turn out all right,"
I didn't believe a word they said.
I remember God—and shake my head.
I bow my head—then wring my hands.
I'm awake all night—not a wink of sleep;
I can't even say what's bothering me.
I go over the days one by one,
I ponder the years gone by.
I strum my lute all through the night,
wondering how to get my life together.
Will the Lord walk off and leave us for good?
Will he never smile again?
Is his love worn threadbare?
Has his salvation promise burned out?
Has God forgotten his manners?
Has he angrily stomped off and left us?
"Just my luck," I said. "The High God retires
just the moment I need him."
Once again I'll go over what God has done,
lay out on the table the ancient wonders;
I'll ponder all the things you've accomplished,
and give a long, loving look at your acts.

Psalms 77: 2-12

Open Wound!

I have a sister in the Lord who has been struggling for a long time with a wound in the physical sense that will not heal and keeps getting reinfected. I know this is perplexing and perpetuating to her and her spouse. Many months, and into years they have struggled to get help to heal this wound and it is hard to understand why God hasn't healed her. I have other friends who struggle with emotional wounds that are open and won't heal. These are just as problematic if not more. In this chapter of Psalms, David is afflicted with depression and he is fighting it without understanding it. He describes it as an open wound-full of despair and he couldn't sleep or even describe what was bothering him. In this place, he questions God's existence and ability to be God. Often we get in places of desperation that are open wounds in our lives which fester and grow in negative germs that permeate us to the point of being filled with stench. This negativity is contagious to others and dangerous. The song writer continues that when he was in this place of deep despair, he turned to his instrument and began to strum and hum. This is important to us because we can realize that he has created a habit of worship. In his desperate circumstances, he turned to his habit and began to strum. The habit changed his heartsong. Listen to that again. Watch what happened. As he began to play and hum, his heart tuned to God again. He began to recount His blessings and there he found the lift from the miry place of depression. Although I didn't include the rest of the song here for conciseness, once he turns his heart tune on, the rest of the song is uplifting God for His goodness. Dark places and circumstances can get us down and discourage us even to the point of depression, but if we make a habit of praise, a habit of worship and a habit of reading His word while praying, then our heart tune will come on again as a piano in the hand of a master tuner. Questioning God isn't a sin. Questioning His goodness or His ability doesn't lessen Him. These places of life come. Tune. Just begin to create a heart habit so that when these times come, the habit of humming and worshiping, prayer and seeking can lift you and hold you. Let my heart song sing for you Jesus.

Taken aback, Jesus addressed the accompanying crowd: "I've yet to come across this kind of simple trust anywhere in Israel, the very people who are supposed to know about God and how he works." When the messengers got back home, they found the servant up and well.

They all realized they were in a place of holy mystery, that God was at work among them. They were quietly worshipful—and then noisily grateful, calling out among themselves, "God is back, looking to the needs of his people!" The news of Jesus spread all through the country. In the next two or three hours Jesus healed many from diseases, distress, and evil spirits. To many of the blind he gave the gift of sight. Then he gave his answer: "Go back and tell John what you have just seen and heard:

The blind see,
The lame walk,
Lepers are cleansed,
The deaf hear,
The dead are raised,
The wretched of the earth
have God's salvation hospitality extended to them.
"Is this what you were expecting?
Then count yourselves fortunate!"

Luke 7: 9-10, 16-17, 21-23

Holy Mystery!

I am writing this for the second time because in my celebration of His authority, I deleted the writing accidentally! Today is a day of celebration of freedom like no other! I am bubbling over although I started writing this from a place of pain and now I am writing it from a place of Holy Mystery! What is Holy Mystery? It is a place of quiet worship that becomes a noisy gratefulness. In this chapter of Luke, we see the Holy Mystery at work first in the faith of the Roman commander who never met Jesus and yet Jesus declared him a man of simple faith. He surprised Jesus with his acceptance of His authority. He was a man who understood authenticity and authority on command. The simple word was enough. Jesus was willing to prove Himself to this man and yet this man accepted His authority sight unseen-by reputation alone. Jesus heals. The politicians and Jewish leaders were groveling before this man of authority and went to Jesus on his behalf. Jesus agreed to go heal the man's servant as asked but when the commander found out that Jesus was taking the time to travel that way, he sent word that there was no need as he understood Jesus' authority. Grasp this! We need to find this place of Holy mystery in our own lives. We need to begin to walk in the Holy mystery so that our quiet worship becomes a ground swell of noisy gratefulness that takes our countries by storm. We need to grasp that His authority has no limitations of place or person but is here in us. When we get hold of this, the noisy gratefulness will be more than a media report about a quiet worship but will be full of healings and testimonies. When the people around Jesus realized that they were walking in Holy mystery, the quiet worship became a noisy celebration of freedom louder than any fireworks and spread throughout the country getting attention. John sent someone to ask Jesus if He was the Messiah. Jesus answered by more...more healings, more wonders, more deliverances, and more raised from the dead. Jesus was motivated and inspired by the worship of the Holy Mystery. Then He asked, "Is this what you were expecting? Then count yourselves fortunate!" Grasp this! We, the wretched of this Earth have had God's salvation hospitality extended to us! We have His authority extended to us! Start quietly celebrating His goodness, His faithfulness. Begin to focus on His salvation to us then watch how your spirit swells in a grateful noise of celebration of His authority. The news of Jesus at work in us will spread through the whole country when we realize His authority is over all. There is no sickness, disease, chronic conditions or pains that are not subject to His authority. His stripes give us healings. He asks us, is this salvation hospitality what you were expecting...then count yourselves fortunate! Start celebrating Him! Begin in quiet worship to tell Him of your gratefulness then watch that gratitude swell into the Holy mystery of His presence and authority in our lives so that we too walk in healing and wholeness! There is nothing too big for our God! Lord, we are grateful for you! Jesus, today we celebrate our freedom in you! We delight in the salvation hospitality that is extended to us and we walk in Holy Mystery of your authority over all that impacts our lives! Sickness, can stay no longer for your perfect love has cast it out! Fear is gone because you are the Light of Life that dispels it into outer darkness! You Lord have all authority over ALL!

He said, "You've been given insight into God's kingdom—you know how it works. There are others who need stories. But even with stories some of them aren't going to get it: Their eyes are open but don't see a thing, Their ears are open but don't hear a thing.

Then he said to his disciples, "Why can't you trust me?" They were in absolute awe, staggered and stammering, "Who is this, anyway? He calls out to the winds and sea, and they do what he tells them!" Jesus said, "Daughter, you took a risk trusting me, and now you're healed and whole. Live well, live blessed!"

Luke 8: 10, 25, 48

Risking Trust!

True trust is risky as it requires vulnerability. I see this every day as clients come to me with their learning issues and open up enough to allow us to work with them to change their thinking processes. It is scary to trust especially when you have been hurt a lot or recently. As Jesus shares with the people following Him, we are given insight that it isn't just His disciples with Him but lots of people. In fact, many times, He and those with Him are blessed and served by at least three women who are mentioned in this chapter as being women of means who gave. As He relates parables and stories, His disciples ask why and He informs them that He uses stories to express certain thoughts that are hard to grasp to give insight to others. He does this with me each morning and I share. The nugget today is about taking the risk of trust. Trusting God is not a one time thing. It is moment by moment. It is a continuous choice. Like love, trust is a vulnerable opening into a person's soul-their personal space and heart. If the soul isn't open, the eyes can look but not see and the ears can hear but not listen. We see in this chapter that even those closest to Him didn't get Him while in the boat during the storm. They didn't understand who He truly is just as we often fail to realize it when our boat of life is feeling like it is capsizing. We holler out-God, we are about to drown here...and He says, Why can't you trust me? Then as the storm waves begin to subside, we look in wonder as we forgot who He is. This is why Jesus recognized the touch on the hem of His garment which healed the sweet widow with the issue of blood. In that culture, blood was unclean. The truth is she could've had colon cancer, or any number of things which caused this condition. In the setting of time, people with blood issues had to stay away from others and declare themselves unclean until the bleeding stopped. This was important to cleanliness and prevention of disease. Understandable that she took a risk because her life had been on hold for years! It was a huge risk that could've resulted in bad things for her but she was at a place of desperation. Desperation makes our vulnerability less scary and we are more open to risk then. Jesus told her that her vulnerability and willingness to take that risk is the faith that healed her. She was willing to bet it all, even her very life on Him. Walking in faith requires the vulnerability of trust, not that God can but that He will. It requires being willing to risk the trust without knowing the outcome. It requires the vulnerability of love-true open love without borders or hedges or protections or safe backing up places but a trust that says, you are all I have and I will trust despite the way things look. Trusting through the storm-knowing we are in His safety. Trusting through the challenges knowing that He has a purpose and plan. Trusting through the letdowns and disappointments knowing He has a reason that is being perfected in His perfect will. Being in love with Jesus requires the vulnerability of risking trust. Can we truly see Him, hear Him, trust Him? Only through faithful love. Love shuts down the doubt and fear. Love opens the channel of trust and makes us vulnerable to the faith walk.
This is how we begin to Know God intimately.

Meanwhile, Peter and those with him were slumped over in sleep. When they came to, rubbing their eyes, they saw Jesus in his glory and the two men standing with him. When Moses and Elijah had left, Peter said to Jesus, "Master, this is a great moment! Let's build three memorials: one for you, one for Moses, and one for Elijah." He blurted this out without thinking. While he was babbling on like this, a light-radiant cloud enveloped them. As they found themselves buried in the cloud, they became deeply aware of God. Then there was a voice out of the cloud: "This is my Son, the Chosen! Listen to him."
When the sound of the voice died away, they saw Jesus there alone. They were speechless. And they continued speechless, said not one thing to anyone during those days of what they had seen.

Luke 9: 32-36

Deeply Aware!

"Meanwhile, Peter and those with him were slumped over in sleep. When they came to, rubbing their eyes, they saw Jesus in his glory and the two men standing with him. When Moses and Elijah had left, Peter said to Jesus, "Master, this is a great moment! Let's build three memorials: one for you, one for Moses, and one for Elijah." He blurted this out without thinking. While he was babbling on like this, a light-radiant cloud enveloped them. As they found themselves buried in the cloud, they became deeply aware of God. Then there was a voice out of the cloud: "This is my Son, the Chosen! Listen to him." When the sound of the voice died away, they saw Jesus there alone. They were speechless. And they continued speechless, saying not one thing to anyone during those days of what they had seen. * * *"
Luke 9:32-36 MSG

How often have we missed God's presence because we rushed into a situation before hearing, feeling and sensing Him. Another example of these sleeping disciples in the midst of the presence of God. The scripture says...while he was babbling on...making his man plans and thinking his Earthly thoughts... God formed a rainbow cloud over them, around them, a hush cloud...then He spoke. How often in communion with God do we find the need to babble on and on when He is there in our presence waiting? These few disciples that were close to Jesus often missed out on great things because they allowed their flesh to become weak, tired, and absorbed by the day to day. We are just like them. We miss the quiet stillness of His confident presence because we rush about trying to make a certain thing happen in our way. God was there when Peter was asleep and when he awoke. Peter rushed into the moment without taking time to observe the fullness of the situation. Take time. When we take time in prayer and scripture, we become deeply aware of His presence in our lives. He is always present but we are the ones who miss the awareness. God brought a hush cloud down to get Peter's attention and make Him deeply aware of Him because in the day to day, Peter had forgotten who Jesus is/was/will be. Peter got caught up in the majesty moment he awoke to but forgot who it was in that moment. He approached Jesus as a human friend with limited capacity rather than as God. The Holy Hush as Peter and others became deeply aware of God. Today, take time to sit in His presence. Feel Him, experience Him. Be quiet and embrace Him. I love a song that a friend sings so well about sitting at His feet, drinking from the cup in His hand, lying back against Him to breathe and feel His heartbeat. His heart beats for us in love and sacrifice. Isn't it time that we took time to just be quiet in Him? Be still and Know that He is God. Nothing more. He said,"This is My Son, the Chosen. Listen to Him." We cannot hear Him until we listen.

Jesus said, "What a generation! No sense of God! No focus to your lives! How many times do I have to go over these things? How much longer do I have to put up with this? Bring your son here."

Jesus refused. "First things first. Your business is life, not death. And life is urgent: Announce God's kingdom!"

Jesus said, "No procrastination. No backward looks. You can't put God's kingdom off till tomorrow. Seize the day."

Luke 9: 41, 60, 62

God Sense!

Movies are made, books written, podcasts aired, and videos filmed about the "sixth sense" or "seventh sense" which are considered to be interoception/proprioception. These additional senses allow us to keep track of where our body parts are in relation to self; an intuitive feeling to protect ourselves both internally and externally. We are well acquainted with our five senses of taste, smell, feel, see, and hear but we are not as well acquainted by definition with our other senses. We try to define or label our God sense-that inner small voice as intuition or other fancy names when it is our primary sense before all others. Jesus called it our lack of God sense or in older versions "faithless:perverse generation". We prioritize wrong. We put things of Earthly concern before things of God. We worry more about politics and things occurring in that realm rather than being concerned about people. We get more concerned about our physical health than our spiritual wellness. We ponder our feelings and emotions over God's truths. When I was raising my children, I taught them that "happiness" is a choice. You can choose your emotions. It is called emotional regulation. The emotions come as a reaction but we have control over them, they do not control us. Love is a choice. We do not fall in and out of love. That is a lie. Love is a daily or sometimes minute by minute choice just like all other emotions and we must learn to not live in our emotions but to feel them and let them go. Counselors, psychologists, psychiatrists, pastors and many other mental healthcare providers are constantly booked because we as a generation have lost the ability to emotionally regulate as we have become accustomed with letting our self rule instead of growing the fruit of self-control. The number one market in videos, books and all media is self-help. Why? Because we are consumed so much with self, which is flesh backwards. We are lost, faithless and perverse because we have lost our God sense. Our focus is constantly being tested with technology from iPhone to social media. We are consumed with our own pleasure and feelings so much that we have lost the sense of reality. Jesus asks, "How many times does He have to go over this?" He instructs that our business is life, not being consumed with death prevention but God's kingdom life. He says we must seize the day because God's kingdom cannot be put off until tomorrow. These passages in Luke seem harsh. We do not like the idea that our earthly concerns are not the priority. Getting our hair colored or nails done, traveling for vacation or even business are not as important as listening for the voice of God. Worrying about our health and wellness is not as important as being concerned with those who have not heard. God is calling us to use the tools He has provided to be about His business. Political morass and Earthly concerns pale in light to His kingdom like a night-light to the sun. The things that consume us need to be reprioritized. Let the things of God come first and the things of Earth will fall into place. Life is urgent. Time is waning. No backward looks or regrets. March forward into His pursuit and watch the things of Earth line up for His glory. Tune into the God sense that He created in us. To hear a radio station or see a particular app, tv show or other, we must turn it on and tune it in. What if we put away that which distracts us from His purpose and truly turned on God's word and tuned into Him above all else? What if we fully focused on Him in our lives? He is coming soon. Our God sense should be screaming at us that time is short and we must tune in to what He has purposed in us.

"I've been given it all by my Father! Only the Father knows who the Son is and only the Son knows who the Father is. The Son can introduce the Father to anyone he wants to." He then turned in a private aside to his disciples. "Fortunate the eyes that see what you're seeing! There are plenty of prophets and kings who would have given their right arm to see what you are seeing but never got so much as a glimpse, to hear what you are hearing but never got so much as a whisper." The Master said, "Martha, dear Martha, you're fussing far too much and getting yourself worked up over nothing. One thing only is essential, and Mary has chosen it—it's the main course, and won't be taken from her."

Luke 10: 22-24, 41-42

Main Course!

I am a doer. I learned this from my mom. I am constantly doing things for others and I enjoy it. I have been blessed to be a doer but with that gift comes the worry about it all being right. I am a Martha and a Mary...meaning that I often fuss too much over the small things and must be reminded by Him that there is truly only one thing essential to life and that is Him. It is a choice. Sometimes we get so busy serving that we forget who we are doing it for which is the purpose. We get so caught up in the details that we miss the big picture. Jesus said that Only the Father knows the Son and that only the Son knows the Father but the Son can introduce the Father to anyone He wants. He then explains that seeing His example and hearing His words is a treasure that kings and prophets would sacrifice their lives for as it is that high in value. We tend to want to see big miracles of miraculous healings and the big shows of things like the Red Sea parting without realizing the reality that we have already obtained and experienced the biggest miracle of all in salvation. We keep looking for the main course of the Rapture and worrying about His return timing when that is the dessert not the main course. We have already consumed the appetizers of His presence through the Spirit without acknowledgment and often are completely oblivious to this. We have the main course before us daily in so many formats that we fail to appreciate it. The Word is the main course. Salvation is through The Word. In John 1, he tells us In the Beginning was The Word, The Word was with God and The Word Was God.

"The Word was first, the Word present to God, God present to the Word. The Word was God, in readiness for God from day one."John 1:1-2 MSG

This is the main course. The Word that was spoken was God and God became flesh and dwelt among man that He might fulfill the Law spoken by God. He came as The Word. He walked on Earth as The Word. It was His Word that said Let there Be...and it was. It was The Word who healed the broken and did the miracles. It is The Words "It is Finished" which declared the main course for our consumption of salvation. We have the main course in The Word recorded for us in every format from digital to paper and yet, we are so busy fussing and getting worked up about things like Martha that we fail to sit and absorb that which cannot be taken from us like Mary. Have we gotten so busy with doing that we have forgotten The Word? He is patiently waiting. Softly and tenderly calling to us to tune into His presence and feel Him speaking to us. The "doing" is exhausting and wearing. One thing only is essential. Will you choose it?

That's why I don't think there's any comparison between the present hard times and the coming good times. The created world itself can hardly wait for what's coming next. Everything in creation is being more or less held back. God reins it in until both creation and all the creatures are ready and can be released at the same moment into the glorious times ahead. Meanwhile, the joyful anticipation deepens.

Romans 8: 18-21

Held Back!

Anticipation! Nerves, excitement and pent up energy all made their little bodies completely overwhelmed. My boys, as children, had such vivid imaginations and expectations that many times their emotions bubbled over in anticipation of an event from a birthday party to a school field day. Many times, I literally had to grab hold of them and hold them back from rushing into a situation or circumstance, because their whole being could hardly wait. I remember one incident vividly where we sat on the side of the road watching the people line up for the Christmas parade. The parade went right in front of our house. As people lined up, they first had to go past our house to the park where the queue began. My eldest loved horses and a horse-drawn sleigh with Santa came by at that moment. And before you know it, those little legs had taken him on a sprint towards Santa, headed right into the path of an oncoming car. He had eyes only on what he desired and never saw the dangers. As his mom, I saw and I rescued him by grabbing his shirt and holding him back as he wiggled and fussed. I calmly explained to him, but his anticipation was so great that nothing I did was getting through. Suddenly, a different noise got his attention. The parade was beginning. The band had started. He was ready to stand in his chair and see, because he knew the time was finally here. I know there is no comparison in this to the anticipation of what is coming. But in my mind and heart, I feel the festival is ready to begin. The final details are being done. The Bridegroom is walking through the marriage supper room. All creation senses Him and is raring to break loose in celebration, but God Himself reins them in, until all is ready to be released. The sound of the trumpet will signal the call. The midnight cry is joyfully anticipated. Our hearts are eager and ready, but our job is to prepare the way. Jesus will come quickly as a thief in the night. We must prepare ourselves, constantly and consistently checking the details of our lives in anticipation. However, we must not let the expectations and excitement of the moment deter us from the role He has called us to play. Our part in the play is cast. Our lines have been given. The curtain has risen and we are on the stage of life calling out to those in the audience to join us. We must help them see the joyful anticipation that is behind the scenes of the life role we play. If we get too caught up in our role, that we forget this is only a play in anticipation of the final curtain, we lose sight of the full purpose. The circumstances of our lives happen to draw others towards the light of who He is. Do not get distracted by this role. Remember the deep learning and lean into the Master Director for the play is closing soon. Refresh your lines for a last curtain call. Go out on the stage of life and share your anticipation of His return in this final hour. He is coming soon!

"No one lights a lamp, then hides it in a drawer. It's put on a lamp stand so those entering the room have light to see where they're going. Your eye is a lamp, lighting up your whole body. If you live wide-eyed in wonder and belief, your body fills up with light. If you live squinty-eyed in greed and distrust, your body is a musty cellar. Keep your eyes open, your lamp burning, so you don't get musty and murky. Keep your life as well-lighted as your best-lighted room."

Luke 11: 33-36

Musty Cellar!

Dank and dirty, musty and murky is the life that is lived in doubt and distrust. Early this morning, my husband told me to come outside to see something and across the sky was a long line of white blinking dots. In wide eyed wonder, we watched as they traveled quite quickly across the sky in a line. Suddenly, one or two left the line and stayed put for a minute before their lights went out and the others disappeared from view. At first, we thought it was a meteor but there was no tail and it was a line of dots. Upon research, we learned it was an array of SpaceX satellites. Those satellites have been put into place for us to have technologies available to us here on Earth. Jesus said in Luke that when we live a life of openness and wonder like a child who is experiencing something wonderful for the first time, our body fills up with light. He said our eye is a lamp lighting up our whole body and just as a light lights a whole dark room, so these eyes of wonder will keep us lit throughout the dark. Eyes of wonder and belief look for the impossibles to become possibles. I can remember the very first time my boys saw a magic show at the library. They were fascinated and in awe that the magician did impossible things. One little boy kept getting up and running around the magician trying to find the trick. He could not accept the "magic" of the impossible and he was filled with distrust searching for the trick. He missed out on the wonder because he was looking with distrust at every opportunity. God is not a magician who makes the seemingly impossible happen with tricks and skills. God is the God of the possibles that we cannot fathom or imagine. He doesn't comprehend impossible because to Him ALL things are possible. What we look at with our distrust and doubt, fear and insecurity to Him is just a word waiting to be said. He tells us through The Word of His son in this passage in Luke to Keep our lives as well-lit as our best room. I have a chandelier in my house that is huge and beautiful. It is so bright that it has only been turned on a few times a year. The light from it is incredible and spectacular. It lights every corner of my house top to bottom by itself because it is so bright. When I read this today, I thought of that light. It is truly incredible when it is on. We function most of our lives without using it at all because we have other lights but on really dark days/nights when we have people over, that chandelier draws so much wattage and sparkles so much that people can see it from our road. Jesus says we are to live a life of trust and belief like that chandelier in my foyer area. We are to sparkle and shine drawing all the people around us to Him by our shining trust and belief in Him for the impossible. What impossible things are you shining in wonder, waiting for God to do? Have you given up on His promise and gone into the deep dank cellar of unbearable unbelief or are you just needing to turn that light switch on? No matter where you are in life, God is still light and truth. In Him you can trust no matter how dark the situation seems. Daniel trusted from a lion's den and he was saved. Joseph trusted from a pit and a prison, from both he was saved. Esther trusted from a place of child trafficking and was raised up to become queen. Ruth trusted from being a widow and a beggar, then became a mother in the line of kings. Paul trusted from prison, shipwreck, snake bite, torture....he was saved through it all and raised up to glory despite being martyred. Get up and flip on that light switch. If you have wandered into that musty cellar of distrust, let this be a match to light your lantern as you make your way back to the well lit room of trust and belief. Keep watch. Keep your eyes of trust open to see what God will do in the place of your impossible. Watch with wonder and awe as He works a new thing for each of us. It is a choice you make and no other can do it. Will you choose wide-eyed well lit wonder and awe of belief or will you doubt as you walk sinking deeper and deeper into that musty old place of doubt? The choice matters because your light beckons others. The choice matters because eternity awaits. The choice matters because the King of all glory has offered you the Light of the World to share through the sacrifice of His life. What will you do?

God's Word is better than a diamond,
better than a diamond set between emeralds.
You'll like it better than strawberries in spring,
better than red, ripe strawberries.
There's more: God's Word warns us of danger
and directs us to hidden treasure.
Otherwise how will we find our way?
Or know when we play the fool?
Clean the slate, God, so we can start the day fresh!
Keep me from stupid sins,
from thinking I can take over your work;
Then I can start this day sun-washed,
scrubbed clean of the grime of sin.
These are the words in my mouth;
these are what I chew on and pray.
Accept them when I place them
on the morning altar,
O God, my Altar-Rock,
God, Priest-of-My-Altar.

Psalms 19: 10-14

Heavenly Gems!

Diamonds are a girl's best friend or so the saying goes. In Psalms, David reminds us that God's word is the real gem by clearly stating that God's word is better than a diamond set between emeralds as it warns us of dangers and directs us to hidden treasure. I am a treasure hunter, a collector and I do love diamonds but none of these compare to the joy I have when finding a nugget of truth in His word that I can dig into, pull out, polish and see the hidden beauty. In fact, I am infinitely fascinated with the intricacies of His word and how His Spirit reveals new facets each time you explore it. I have written about treasure and diamonds before. I have explored the hidden depths of God's word many times. Every time I dig in, I find treasure. Every time. His word has a depth like no other and a newness and freshness that is incomparable. For many years, I was a jewelry lady on the side. I sold Premier Jewelry and collected a lot of it. None of these pieces had deep value on resale as none of the gems were real. They sparkled and looked pretty. They wore well and enhanced but none of them had true lasting value. A few of the pieces have special value to me as one necklace is a depiction of Heaven, another has scriptures and a mustard seed in glass which are reminders much like the bracelets that are etched with affirmations from God's word. As I was cleaning out, I noticed I had amassed an incredible amount of this jewelry and enjoyed it but in doing so, the pieces of jewelry I owned that had true lasting value with real gemstones like diamonds and rubies were put aside because they were not as large or ostentatious. Initially, it was because I was selling the jewelry that it took the place of the pieces of true lasting value. Then it was because I didn't want to lose my valuable jewelry, so I hid it away. Then it was because in the amassing, it was easier, because I could no longer easily find the pieces with true value. I hope you can see what I am saying. The things of God become hidden treasure, often because of us. God makes it plain to us in His word. It is clearly written and has depth and value every time but we acquire other things to help us understand His word. Then we begin to amass these other things in our lives until we find we have such an overwhelming place of acquisition that we can no longer find that peace of true value. We have hidden the truth under wraps of layers of life and spent so much time serving Him and doing things of life that those diamonds have become hidden treasures mounted in a beautiful setting between emeralds but buried under mounds of other stuff in our lives. It is time to clear the clutter. It is time to find those pieces of true value and depth. Uncovering the facets of beautiful diamonds of His word by clearing our lives of the clutter and polishing His gems of truth, allows the brilliance of His word to once again take hold and have flavor in our lives. David says it will taste better than red, ripe, juicy strawberries in spring. Feeling hungry? Ready for a treasure hunt to uncover the gems of God's word? These are the gateway to His promises in our lives. He has given us the treasure map and all the answers we need. It is time to dig in and discover these Heavenly Gems of His words that exude power and can be placed upon the Altar of our lives opening the portals of Heavenly purpose to us. These are where true value lies. The clutter is cleared, the treasures revealed, now we must begin to wear His word around our neck as a beacon of glittering gems that sits in radiant settings drawing others to Him. The old song says, "Sing them over again to me, beautiful words, wonderful words, wonderful words of life. Let me more of His beauty see, wonderful words of life."

"I've never, as you so well know, had any taste for wealth or fashion. With these bare hands I took care of my own basic needs and those who worked with me. In everything I've done, I have demonstrated to you how necessary it is to work on behalf of the weak and not exploit them. You'll not likely go wrong here if you keep remembering that our Master said, 'You're far happier giving than getting.'"

Acts 20: 33-35

Basic Needs!

A few of my LearningRx graduates have now gone on to military duty and a couple have just completed basic training and were on my mind this morning as I read my scriptures and began to pray. God spoke clearly to me that basic training in Him is what is lacking in so many. You see in basic training, the purpose is to break down the dependency factor and rebuild the person without breaking the will. Tough love. Through intense exercise, the body is broken down and exhausted but rebuilt as this brings about good self-discipline. Through isolation from familiar contacts, the dependency on others is broken down and rebuilt into a dependency only on God and hearing/understanding purposes of those instructions from those in charge. From sleep deprivation, the mind is broken down from emotional dependence so that one relies on orders and not emotions. Our basic needs for safety, nutrition and care are taken care of when we begin to realize that the other things we see as necessary are really only distractions. When we get down to basic needs, we begin to realize truths about ourselves and find our true depths. We do not have to go to boot camp to do this. We can do as Paul instructs and work hard with our own hands and abilities to care for ourselves and others. We can work on behalf of the weak and not exploit them. As my husband has gone about doing tree work for people after this storm, he has been amazed at how many are being taken advantage of in this way. His prices are fair but about 1/10th of what others are charging and people came from all over like ants looking to exploit those who were in need after the storm. This is wrong! Paul instructs us as he does the church that exploitation of others is not of God. We are to do all we can to get back to the true basics of life. This is a pure heart in love with God and His word. We must discipline ourselves to time in prayer and studying His word so that when the tests of life come, we can stand strong rather than failing. Our life will live right when we get back to the basics and away from the frivolous. The basics of a pure heart and right living come from establishing that He is all we need. Get away. Put your mind only on Him then begin to see what He desires for you!

He wants not only us but everyone saved, you know, everyone to get to know the truth we've learned: that there's one God and only one, and one Priest-Mediator between God and us—Jesus, who offered himself in exchange for everyone held captive by sin, to set them all free. Eventually the news is going to get out. This and this only has been my appointed work: getting this news to those who have never heard of God, and explaining how it works by simple faith and plain truth.

1 Timothy 2: 4-7

Plain Truth!

Simple faith and plain truth seems like such an easy concept, and yet we complicate it. God only wants us to lead others to the Lord, so that everyone is saved and everyone gets to learn the truth. This truth is that we know there is only one God, and only one priest, one mediator between God and us, and his name is Jesus. He offered Himself in exchange for everyone through His sacrifice on the cross. This news is incredible news! And yet so many want to take this message and make it complicated with rules of behavior and dress, and so many other factors. The simple truth is that Jesus saves just because we accept it in simple faith. Through that salvation, He then brings about restoration and sanctification. Those things are not our job. Yes, we are to mentor and help people grow closer to God and yes, we are to help them to see when there are errors in their ways in a loving approach. But it is not our job to criticize and put down and make things hard. This has given the church a bad name and a bad reputation. Living under rules and things that are there to put people down is not why Jesus came. In fact, the Pharisees and Sadducees ruled the people of the day when Jesus came. They were the people who tried Jesus. These people are truly all about self. They are not of God, because being of God means that He takes first priority and getting his word out to everyone no matter what is first priority. So many get caught up in the politics of religion and the church, that they miss out on the simple, plain truth of faith bringing about salvation. In Timothy, this message is plainly laid out so that any could see. This does not erase that true salvation brings about change. Salvation and acceptance of the gift that Jesus gave through the sacrifice of His life for our sins means that we are ready to put self away and live for Him. If we live for Him and only Him, then our lives will reflect that we live for Him and only Him. This message should not be complicated but true. If someone lives in sin darkness, then is shown the light, they can decide to turn towards it and begin walking in it towards the fullness of freedom or to turn away. That is the choice. Fullness of light life only comes by walking in it and towards that fullness. There are many Christians all along this path of light. Some have just seen the Light and are turning while others have been walking in that fullness for a while as they edge ever closer to His goodness and faithfulness. It is a different path that we each walk. No one walks it exactly the same as we must all work out our own salvation in Him through respect for who He is and awe at what He has done for us. Let's get our mind set that it is our job to show the light and guide but not to push or shove lest we step into the darkness of deception ourselves. We are all in a cave of sin in this world and we choose to walk in His light towards the Higher calling to Freedom and Eternal Life. At no point, is it our job to leave the Light and wander into darkness to call others. We are to take the light and show others to the Source of the Light, then let Him do the revealing of the darkness in their lives. Preach the Simple Truth, share in faithful love and lead to Him. This is simple faith and plain truth that I was once lost but now I am found. I can walk in the Light of His love because He set me free and gives me the opportunities to share in His glorious presence daily. Drawing others to Him is like drawing moths to a flame. All we must do is be open and truthful while walking in His light and allow Him to draw through us.

God appeared to Solomon that very night and said, "I accept your prayer; yes, I have chosen this place as a temple for sacrifice, a house of worship. If I ever shut off the supply of rain from the skies or order the locusts to eat the crops or send a plague on my people, and my people, my God-defined people, respond by humbling themselves, praying, seeking my presence, and turning their backs on their wicked lives, I'll be there ready for you: I'll listen from heaven, forgive their sins, and restore their land to health. From now on I'm alert day and night to the prayers offered at this place. Believe me, I've chosen and sanctified this Temple that you have built: My Name is stamped on it forever; my eyes are on it and my heart in it always. As for you, if you live in my presence as your father David lived, pure in heart and action, living the life I've set out for you, attentively obedient to my guidance and judgments, then I'll back your kingly rule over Israel—make it a sure thing on a sure foundation. The same covenant guarantee I gave to David your father I'm giving to you, namely, 'You can count on always having a descendant on Israel's throne.'

2 Chroicles 7: 12-18

Attentively Obedient!

"As for you, if you live in my presence as your father David lived, pure in heart and action, living the life I've set out for you, attentively obedient to my guidance and judgments, then I'll back your kingly rule over Israel—make it a sure thing on a sure foundation. The same covenant guarantee I gave to David your father I'm giving to you."

God's promise held true for the reign of Solomon as his reign is still known as the richest and most prosperous time of rule. Not only that, but because he asked for wisdom and not riches, he got both. The key that unlocked God's promise was attentive obedience. Mindless obedience is doing something out of habit rather than careful working. Attentive obedience requires attention to the details. Lots of people use this scripture and promise in mindless ways. They quote "if my people, called by my name, will humble themselves and pray, I will heal their land". This is the promise but the promise comes with a requirement or key to operating in God's promise. That is the "if" of attending to God's will. The humbling process isn't fun. It is a laying down of my own hopes, desires and dreams with complete trust that God's way is better. The rest of the promise says that they must humble themselves, pray, seek God's presence and turn from their own wicked ways, then and only then will God be ready to listen, forgive and restore. We are like the little kid who wants the reward but also wants to act however we desire to act. We want things to go our way in our time. Here's a thing to consider. In any situation, there is a possibility of two praying people who are both humble and righteous, praying for opposite things. I think of the recent storms and the blessings of provision that they have brought into our lives through the mess and cleanup. We were praying that God send my husband work and jobs as his business has been struggling. God sent work and has provided but I know during that storm and before, people were praying for it to not be bad. We didn't pray for the storm to come. We prayed for God's hand to move mightily on our behalf. That doesn't always look like we think it will look. The knowing of God is in the intimacy of attending Him in obedience. He said "if you live in my presence, pure in heart and action, living the life I have set out for you, attentively obedient to my guidance and judgment, then I will make your life a sure thing on a sure foundation." God's promises are true and lasting. The actions are ours to choose. It requires us to pay attention to what He is doing and respond when He instructs us. Sure foundational promises await our choice to pay attention to His call.

**God's name is a place
of protection–
good people can run there
and be safe.
Wise men and women are
always learning,
always listening for fresh insights.
Find a good spouse, you find a
good life–
and even more:
the favor of God!**

Proverbs 18: 10, 15, 22

Best Advice!

Lots of things are going through my mind today as I opened His word. These nuggets of advice jumped out at me from Proverbs. Note that I did read the whole chapter and there were lots of great pieces of advice but these were my takeaways for today. God's name is a place of shelter and comfort no matter what trial has come our way. He is a place of protection but His name alone has more power than anything in the Earth. His name protects and guards us from the enemy as a strong tower. Now, how do you run to a name alone for protection? In situations that we struggle, we can call on His mighty name to reign in the powers of the enemy. I remember when my boys were small and something scared them, they would holler out "Momma" and then run towards me. Nothing could've stopped me from protecting them with all I had-mama bear syndrome. God is all powerful and His name holds all resources and power. This may be a fresh insight for you as it is for me. This passage says that wise men and women are always learning and listening for fresh insights. We are blessed with an infinite amount of knowledge at our fingertips nowadays so we can learn new things but we must remember that much of history and experience is not recorded but learned by listening to those who can recount it with accuracy. I enjoy watching my parents interact for this reason. I learn and listen to them as they interact. They have found the favor of God and a good life in each other as they have become. I look at my own spouse and see how blessed I am that God sent me a good man who has provided a good life and more as we live in the favor of God. Does this mean we do not have troubles? Not at all. We have had some doozies! But we know that together we can call on the name of God and run into His presence for safety, shelter and delivery from all that is sent our way. We listen and learn together in His presence for insight from His word. We bind together in His name in situations that would take so many down, trusting that He will work a good work in us. I encourage you to read His word and learn from Him for fresh insight. I encourage you to seek a good life from Him by calling upon His name.

I encourage you to encourage one another in the love of God. If you have found a good spouse, then go together to the house of God and learn. Run to Him together in times of trouble and listen always for fresh insight. If you have not yet found a good spouse or your spouse has gone before you into eternity, I encourage you to embrace Who He Is in the good times and the dark valleys. If you have been let down by life, including a spouse or loved one, I encourage you to run to His name. Run to Him. He is father to fatherless and spouse to those who have lost or hurting. Whatever it is, take it to Him as simply as calling His name. Then listen and learn from His word. Dig out the nuggets He has for you. They are the best advice.

"But be on your guard. Don't let the sharp edge of your expectation get dulled by parties and drinking and shopping. Otherwise, that Day is going to take you by complete surprise, spring on you suddenly like a trap, for it's going to come on everyone, everywhere, at once. So, whatever you do, don't fall asleep at the wheel. Pray constantly that you will have the strength and wits to make it through everything that's coming and end up on your feet before the Son of Man."

Luke 21: 34-36

On Guard!

The bees swarmed suddenly all around his machine but the windows were buttoned up tight and they could do nothing but batter at the windows. Mowing a field comes with the unexpected but my husband expected things to fly up, not for bees to surround. Evidently he had hit not one but two hives hidden in the ground. The sharp edge of the blade cut through the grass and all other, leaving a clean field with bees swarming everywhere. He was caught off guard and surprised but his machine was enclosed so he was protected. This is exactly what Luke recorded Jesus saying in this passage about the last days. We are going about our business of the day to day but He alerts us to not allow our sharpness and preparedness be dulled by the day to day or we will be caught off guard, surprised and trapped by the suddenness of these events that precede Jesus' return. He instructs us to pray constantly that we will have our wits and strength to make it through the things that are coming and end up on our feet before Him. He said many will fall asleep on the way, allowing their senses to be dulled by drink and their lifestyle. He warns us to stay in prayer. It is so easy to get caught up in our day to day and to let our guard down. Even easier is to not work to keep ourselves sharp in His word because there is a plethora of songs, books, podcasts, videos, etc. It is so much easier to listen or worship at another's behest or leading but God is calling us to sharpen our own abilities and keep ourselves honed to His word through prayer and praise. We must seek His will and not our own. Cleaning, caring, sharpening and preparing all required work they require us to be busy in His purpose. The signs of the Time are everywhere, and we must be about the business of preparing our guard for many deceivers, and much is out there that will lead us down a wrong path. Lean in, get your guard up in prayer and strengthen His will in your life by honing yourselves in prayer.

Who out there fears God,
actually listens to the voice of his servant?
For anyone out there who doesn't know where
you're going,
anyone groping in the dark,
Here's what: Trust in God.
Lean on your God!
But if all you're after is making trouble,
playing with fire,
Go ahead and see where it gets you.
Set your fires, stir people up,
blow on the flames,
But don't expect me to just stand
there and watch.
I'll hold your feet to those flames.

Isaiah 50: 10-11

Trust & Lean!

In verse 4 of Isaiah 50, the author penned words that echoed in my heart this morning: "The Master God has given me a well-taught tongue so I know how to encourage tired people." If you are struggling today, don't know the next step, have no idea where you are going and feel like you are groping in the dark, here's what and where: Trust God! Lean on God! These words seem mighty easy to say but hard to do when you are in the dark. I want to witness from personal experience that He is true in the deepest of depths and the darkest of places. When you are feeling the grips of an impossible situation, when the trial is burning hot and those around you seem to fan the flames to be immune to your discomfort, then it is truly time to lean in. How does one lean in when they are groping in the darkness? The answer is by simply beginning to praise. The fear or respect for God brings wisdom and His praise is like no other. When your spirit praises, it's behind the process to unlock the impossible. It breaks down walls like in Jericho and prison doors like it did for Paul & Silas. Praise is the key to the treasured heart of God. He inhabits the praise of His people as the psalmist said. He delights in the praises of His people and He desires to do all things good for those who serve Him in righteousness. These are His promises that we lean into while groping in the dark, lost and wandering through the impossible situations. He is a friend who sticks closer than a brother and He is able to do exceedingly and abundantly more than we ask or think. All we must do to unlock the doors and windows of His heart towards us is praise. The power of praise is a mighty force that encourages change. It changes our mindset from woe is me to how great is God. When our mind is no longer centered on our selfish ways and desires, our needs are met, managed and abundantly blessed by He who is more than enough. If we don't understand, all we need to do is hold His hand in praise because He has all things in His control.

But you are the ones chosen by God, chosen for the high calling of priestly work, chosen to be a holy people, God's instruments to do his work and speak out for him, to tell others of the night-and-day difference he made for you—from nothing to something, from rejected to accepted.

1 Peter 2: 9-10

God Chosen!

What a privilege it is to be chosen to represent the highest calling! In olden days, this calling was for a very select few who held to the highest standard of law. With the advent of Jesus and His supreme sacrifice as the High Priest of Himself the perfect lamb, spotless and pure, we are called directly to the duty or priestly work. We are called to be His instruments to do His work and speak out for Him. We are called to live a life set apart so that we can tell others of the difference He has made for us. We are called to show how we came from nothing to something and from rejected to accepted. We are called and chosen. I know when I awake in pain and body aches that I do not feel called or chosen but that is the pressure of this world upon this earthly inhabitant. The calling is an eternal call upon the soul and it is through the rejoicing that the overcoming happens. Our flesh is weak and may fail but God is strong and will not fail. We must remember the calling, the choosing when the days of trouble are upon us. There are all kinds of instruments in life with many different purposes. Some instruments are beautiful serving pieces and others are talented writing pieces, some make beautiful music and other make beautiful art, whichever instrument we are, we must remember that we are His and are called to be used by Him. My pastor says we are pieces of pipe that His blessings, Anointing and words flow through. Whatever type of instrument you are, God has chosen you and is developing you into a very special and sacred piece. A pencil in my hand is just a writing instrument but in the hand of another creates beautiful art. God has called each of us to use our talents for Him. Your talent might be bringing a smile to faces, shining His love in darkness, helping a wayward soul or picking others up from where they are. These talents are God given gifts. Don't let anyone or anything take this gift from you. We are His and in His hand, we are instruments He uses to create masterpieces.

Hallelujah!
You who serve God, praise God!
Just to speak his name is praise!
Just to remember
God is a blessing—
now and tomorrow and always.
From east to west, from dawn
to dusk, keep lifting all your
praises to God!

Psalms 113: 3

Keep Lifting!

When God wants you to know something, He not only writes it to your heart but He demonstrates it to you again and again. This week has been a resounding echo about the power of praise. Praise carries a current of change as it is the currency of Heaven. We get caught up in the currency of money here on Earth especially when things are hard financially but Jesus showed us with His life to not go about with a care for money. In fact it was the love of money that caused His betrayal by Judas and it is the love of money that causes much betrayal in our world. But money, while being an aspect of our life we must have...it is not the currency that brings true change. The currency of true change is praise. When our lives revolve around our pocketbook, we get bogged down by making the dollar at the sacrifice of other things. Family suffers, lives suffer, our spiritual life suffers because money doesn't hold true power. It is only a false sense of security. But this isn't about money. This is about the power of praise. The psalmist penned it well when he said that those who serve God, praise God. He reminds us that just speaking His name is praise and we should remember the blessing that He is to our lives always. There is no problem too big for God to solve but we must first get our mindset right. We must begin to walk in the power of praise for that is what carries the current of change. This is the place where blessings flow. Currents in the world are seen in the sky as we watch the days/nights change. Currents are in the oceans that carry life from one pole to another and we see the currents in the waves. Currents in storms are seen and heard as lightning and thunder that bring the winds of change. Praise is The current of change. If we desire change and to see God as more than enough, then we must begin to walk in the power of praise. Praise Him in the storms, in the good times, in the bad times, from your place of bondage and in freedom. Praise unlocks prison doors of sickness, disease, finances, emotional health, etc. When we operate in the natural, we experience only what is available in the Earth but when we operate in praise, we experience what only God can do. Praise is as simple or complex as you like. It can be the whisper of His name or the dance of joy. It can be in the delight of His word or in the song from our hearts. The point is do not allow the pressures of this Earth to rob us of our joy which is only found in Him. Praise changes circumstances as the current changes landscapes. The more praise, the more change. I started by telling you how God resounds things to our hearts. Let me emphasize. On Sunday, I attended a different church for a baby dedication and the message was on the God who is more than enough as He inhabits our praise. On Monday, a sister in God sent me a text message about praising God through the hard times. Yesterday a client shared how God changed her life through praise. I was asked to review a book by a colleague that was about abundance through praise. Then today God awoke me with this verse about His blessings through praise. It is surrounding me. The power of praise is a mindset shift for many, but it is the currency of Heaven, for God Himself inhabits the praises of His people. Want More of God? Then start praising and keep praising. Need things to change? Start praising and stay at it. Financial struggles? Begin to call on Heaven's currency through praise so the windows of Heaven pour out abundantly. The power of praise-praise God through whom all blessings flow...praise The Father, The Son and the Holy Ghost. He wants all creation to praise Him and every rock will cry out His praise. Today is a day of change-through the power of praise. Change our mindsets God through the praises from your people.

God rescued us from dead-end
alleys and dark dungeons. He's set us up in the kingdom of the Son he loves so much, the Son who got us out of the pit we were in, got rid of the sins we were doomed to keep repeating.

Colossians 1: 13-14

Dark Dungeons!

Rescued...from the choice, from the pit, from the situation, from uncertainty, from fear, from failure, from heartbreak, from grief...so many times He has rescued me. When I think about His love and how many times He has reached out to rescue me from the things I keep doing, places I keep putting myself in and situations that are of my own making, I am flabbergasted by His love and faithfulness. As Paul stated once, I am amongst the worst of sinners, yet Christ still died for me to rescue me because He loves me. Every day, I am fascinated by the creatures we end up rescuing from our pool. They wander in the dark into the pool and by morning, we must rescue them. For some it is too late as they spent too long in there, treading water and gave up or others absorbed too much of the pool chemistry into their bodies and cannot make it. Still, there are others that are rescued over and over because no matter how many times we pull them out, they continue to fly back towards the water and then become overwhelmed when they cannot get back out. One day, I rescued a particularly strange looking bug 4-5 times in a few minutes' time because every time I got him out of the pool, he immediately turned and went back in. Finally I gave up and before the hour of pool time was over he had expired. Thus, the dead-end alley for him was a place that he was bound and determined to be something more, but each time failed him until he gave up and expired. Thankfully, God doesn't give up on us. He does more than just rescuing us from our pits of despair, He sets us up in the Kingdom of the Son who loves us so much that He gave His life for us. He rescued us from the doom of repeated sin which had the wages of death. Instead He gifted us eternal life through him. I am not a big Star Wars Fan like our friend Charles is but this scripture picture made me think of Charles as I made it. I can just see it scrolling across the screen of life...God rescued us from dead-end alleys and dark dungeons...I can hear the music...He set us up, rescued, freed us from doom. He is the Life Force that is with us. His word is better than a lightsaber, stronger than any weapon formed against us. He got rid of the sins we were doomed to repeat. What a powerful and awesome God He is! God is bigger than.,,,, fill in the blank. He has rescued you and I from it all!

Spirit Warfare!
Ephesians 6:13-18

What are the weapons that we have access to and need when facing our fiercest battles?

_____ is an indispensable weapon. In the same way _____ is essential in this ongoing warfare.

Are you ready for battle?

Key thought for today:

Upset Awe!
Mark 5:16-17

Will you be like those who lost sight of the miracle worker and asked Him to leave or will you hold onto the dream through the circumstances knowing Who He Is?

What will you do with Jesus despite your reality?

Key thought for today:

Tied Up!
Mark 6:4-6

God of the Impossible only stands out when the Impossible is there. Why?

Have you limited God to a box and a timeline? Isn't it time to yield your stubbornness to His strength and get out of His way?

Key thought for today:

Fruit Bearers!
John 15:9-17

Root command =

What is it that God wants us to feel in His love?

How do we become fruit bearers?

Key thought for today:

Dead End!

Isaiah 43:2

GPS =

Do you feel like you have reached a dead end and your life raft is taking on water? Read His promises and be confident that when you are in over your head, He is there with you.

Key thought for today:

Character Soil!
Mark 4:14-20

Word =

Soil =

Why is it important for us to prepare our soul soil with the Living Water?

Have you allowed the gravel of life to become a rocky surface so that you live from emotional high experience to emotional lows? Perhaps it is time to move some gravel out?

Have you gotten so caught up in the cares that life brings that you are choking out what God is doing in your life?

Key thought for today:

Untying Knots!
Mark 4:33-34, 39-40

Why in the face of storms do we so easily lose hope and dive into fear?

Do you need some time in the Father's lap today?

Key thought for today:

Heart Pollution!
Mark 7:18-23

Are you caught up in doing the "right" thing, ignoring the truth in your heart?

What are you focused on, yourself and what you want/desire, or on Him and His purpose so that He can pour through you pure life of Living Water?

Key thought for today:

Miraculous Hint!

Mark 8:11-12, 16-21, 29

Who is He?

Why is it so easy for us to trust that a piece of metal filled with people and an engine can get up into the air, transport us hundreds of miles safely and land but we cannot trust God's timely provisions?

Key thought for today:

Directed Energy!
Galatians 5:22-24

When we truly live God's way, does that mean we won't have times of difficulty?

Why?

Are you fully yielded to Him, allowing Him to make you all He wants you to be?

Key thought for today:

Soaked Clean!
Psalms 51:7-15

Have you allowed your walk with God to become soiled or unyielding to what He is doing?

What can you do to allow the fresh wind of His presence "soak" you clean?

Key thought for today:

Off Base!
Mark 12:24-27

Why do we choose so often to fight in carnal warfare instead of spiritual?

It's easy to fatigue in the game of life, get stuck or discouraged, what are we as Christ followers called to do?

Key thought for today:

See, Hear, Act!
Romans 10:17

Our trials are not for our sake alone but to help others stand when the impossible shakes their world. What are we to do?

Where do we gain trust when the earthquakes riot our lives?

Key thought for today:

Bone Weary!

Galatians 6:9

"Sometimes the uncertainty can be super scary and unstable feeling, but even that can be God directing. The impossible can be a platform to greatness if we "allow ourselves" to continue in His ways despite our current circumstances."

So, what is the key to opening His perfect will for us?

Key thought for today:

Worry Weight!
Proverbs 12:25-26

We all have a "God-sized" hole that only He can fill. When we are not content and full of Him, the empty spot begins to fill with worry.

So, how do we combat worry when it is such a natural emotion to we humans?

Key thought for today:

Counting On!
Micah 7:7-10

When you are going through a tough situation, who/what is the one thing that you can turn to and know that they/it will be there for you no matter what?

Why is it key to have an internal strength in the word of God?

Key thought for today:

Staying Power!
Mark 13:9-13

What are we as "truth sentinels" supposed to do?

God's truth is -

Key thought for today:

Falling Apart!
Mark 14:27-28, 35-36

"Jesus told His disciples and through them, us, that we would feel like our world was falling apart and that it is God's fault. He knew we would reach a place of putting our hand in it, destroying His creation and blaming Him."
How did Jesus prepare and show us the way out?

What/How will you pray today?

Key thought for today:

Alert Expectancy!
Romans 5:1-5

What or where is your "marketplace of ministry"?

Are you allowing God to use you as a vessel of His anointing?

Key thought for today:

Stubborn Unbelief!
Mark 16:14-16

Why is it so easy to believe that our words travel through unseen spaces to another device but so difficult to believe that God, who created all things, including the air we breathe, can intervene in our hard places?

Do we want to be taken to task most severely by God for our unbelief?

Isn't it time we begin to trust and give up our stubborn unbelief so we can be effective tools in His kingdom?

Key thought for today:

Heart Contrast!
Luke 1:19-20, 36-38

When unexpected circumstances arise in your life, how does your heart posture play a role?

What must we do to get our "heart posture" to line up with God's purpose?

Key thought for today:

Post It!
1 Timothy 4:11-14

Each of us has special gifts of ministry that no one else has. What is your "post"?

Are you staying diligently at your "post" or are you allowing doubt to derail you?

Key thought for today:

No Regrets!
Luke 6:35-36

What is the key to living a life of no regrets?

Key thought for today:

Power Up!
Malachi 4:1-6

Sometimes it seems that He has quit working on our behalf but this is not the case. When the trials mount like storms and the days seem endless with frustration, What must we do in order to maintain our 'power"?

Key thought for today:

Look Inside!
2 Corinthians 5:16-20

Are you living and growing in Him, settled to become what He wants you to be or are you rotting and dying inside because you have chosen yourself over His will? Examine it. Embrace the change.

What is a true friend?

He was willing to lay down His life for you. Are you willing to do the same for Him? Look inside.

Key thought for today:

140

Held Deep!
Luke 2:19-20

What do you think would happen if we took more time to ponder what He is doing than to live in the highs and lows?

Do you tend to be like Mary or are you like the shepherds?

Key thought for today:

Failure and Recovery!
Luke 2:25-35

Failure and recovery. Neither of these are fun aspects of life as they both require loss and waiting, patience and fortitude. How can we allow the sorrows of life to become a place of growth in our spiritual lives?

Key thought for today:

Body and Spirit!
Luke 2:46-52

What is the key to being blessed by God and people?

What are we "doing our own way" today instead of being submissively obedient to Him about?

Key thought for today:

Skin Shedding!

Luke 3:7-9

What is your life producing? Are you fruitful and productive or are you deadwood? Are you easily burned up or green and flourishing?

What is your motivation to serve? Are you serving from habit and just skin shedding or are you becoming a new creature in Him? Which are you, snake or caterpillar?

Key thought for today:

Tempting Opportunity!

Luke 4:1-2, 4, 8, 12-13

Temptations and testings are a part of life. They come at unexpected times and certainly come with the intention of deterring us from His purposes. What must we do in order to keep our eyes on the truth?

Key thought for today

Hometown Doom!
Luke 4:23-30

How do people go from being enthralled with God to disgusted with him so quickly? Why is there so little trust, so much lack of faith, and so much frustration with God, when we rarely do our part?

Why do we limit him to what we think he can do or only what we want him to do? Who is God? Is He only what you think and what you want or what I think and I want?

Key thought for today:

Distressed Turn!
2 Corinthians 7:10

When distress and hardships come to tune our life into His ways, why do we allow the distractions and disturbances to pull us out to the deep away from His love?

Why do we fight yielding to His way for our life?

Key thought for today:

Exuberant Earth!

Psalms 27:6-9, 13-14

The Earth recognizes God as the Creator whether man does or doesn't. How do we know this?

For us seeing God's goodness is a choice. Why is it when we are under pressure, we often fail to see that there is value in the process?

Key thought for today:

Authority Simplified!
Luke 5:22-26

We often fail to recognize His authority for what it is, as we walk in the "reality" of life. Why do you think that is?

Why do we make it harder than it has to be when it comes to believing that God can and will answer our prayers?

Key thought for today:

Prayer Pattern!
Luke 6:12-14

When we have struggles or big decisions to make, why do we not just take it to God immediately?

Do you have a special prayer pattern that you always turn to?

Key thought for today:

Royal Advantage!
Philippians 2:5-8

How do we achieve royal advancement?

What are we called to be in a world where privilege reigns?

Key thought for today:

Decisions, Decisions!
Luke 14:28-35

Look at the things dearest to you. Are you willing to lay those things down for His glory?

Are you fully listening to what He is saying to you?

Key thought for today:

Mindset Matters!
Colossians 3:23-24

Evaluate your roles in life. Where are you willing to serve instead of being served?

Are you taking on the mindset of Christ or being selfish in your roles of employment?

Are you busy at work for The Master or too busy complaining about your role in life?

Key thought for today:

Open Wound!
Psalms 77:2-12

What does having a habit of reading His word, praying and praise do for us?

When we are tuned into God, how does this affect our viewpoint on our situations?

Key thought for today:

Holy Mystery!
Luke 7:9-10, 16-17, 21-23

What is Holy Mystery?

Are you fully walking in the Holy Mystery of His authority over all that impacts your life?

Key thought for today:

Risking Trust!

Luke 8:10, 25, 48

Being in love with Jesus requires the vulnerability of risking trust. Can we truly see Him, hear Him, trust Him?

Where is your trust level? Are you willing to risk it all without knowing the outcome?

Key thought for today:

Deeply Aware!
Luke 9:32-36

How often in communion with God do we find the need to babble on and on when He is there in our presence waiting?

Isn't it time that we took time to just be quiet in Him?

Key thought for today:

God Sense!

Luke 9:41, 60, 62

What if we put away that which distracts us from His purpose and truly turned on God's word and tuned into Him above all else? What if we fully focused on Him in our lives?

Key thought for today:

Main Course!
Luke 10:22-24, 41-42

Have we gotten so busy with doing that we have forgotten The Word?

The "doing" is exhausting and wearing. One thing only is essential. Will you choose it?

Key thought for today:

Held Back!

Romans 8:18

The midnight cry is joyfully anticipated. Our hearts are eager and ready, but our job is to prepare the way. Have you been practicing your lines for the last curtain call? Are you prepared to share your anticipation on the stage of life?

Key thought for today:

Musty Cellar!
Luke 11:33-36

What impossible things are you shining in wonder, waiting for God to do?

Have you given up on His promise and gone into the deep dank cellar of unbearable unbelief or are you just needing to turn that light switch on?

Will you choose wide-eyed well lit wonder and awe of belief or will you doubt as you walk sinking deeper and deeper into that musty old place of doubt?

What will you do?

Key thought for today:

Heavenly Gems!

Psalms 19:10-14

Uncovering the facets of beautiful diamonds of His word by clearing our lives of the clutter and polishing His gems of truth, allows the brilliance of His word to once again take hold and have flavor in our lives.David says it will taste better than red, ripe, juicy strawberries in spring. Feeling hungry? Ready for a treasure hunt to uncover the gems of God's word?

Key thought for today:

Basic Needs!
Acts 20:35

What are the basic needs of life?

What must we discipline ourselves to do in order to establish a pure heart and right living?

Key thought for today:

Plain Truth!
1 Timothy 2:5

What is the plain simple truth that God wants each of us to share?

We each walk a different path, what is our job/responsibility with the light?

Key thought for today:

Attentively Obedient!
2 Chronicles 7:12-18

What is the key to unlocking God's promises?

What action will you choose?

Key thought for today:

Best Advice!
Proverbs 18:10, 15, 22

In the midst of troubles, what is the best advice for everyone?

Does living in the favor of God mean we will not have troubles?
What does it mean?

Key thought for today:

On Guard!
Luke 21:34-36

Are you keeping your guard up, staying sharp or are you allowing the things of this world to dull your senses and fall asleep at the wheel?

How does seeking His will help to prepare us and keep us from being caught off guard?

Key thought for today:

Trust and Lean!
Isaiah 50:10-11

How does one lean in when they are groping in the darkness?

How does praising God change our heart?

Key thought for today:

God Chosen!

1 Peter 2:9-10

There are all kinds of instruments in life with many different purposes. What are you doing with yours?

Key thought for today:

Keep Lifting!
Psalms 113:3

Does praise have to be anything more than speaking His name?

What happens when we walk in the power of praise?
What are you waiting for?

Key thought for today:

Dark Dungeons!
Colossians 1:13-14

Thankfully, God doesn't give up on us. He does more than just rescuing us from our pits of despair, He sets us up in the Kingdom of the Son who loves us so much that He gave His life for us. What do you need rescuing from today? Won't you allow God to be your Savior?

Key thought for today:

www.ingramcontent.com/pod-product-compliance
Lightning Source LLC
Chambersburg PA
CBRC090842120626
46551CB00009B/737